THE AIR FORCE
AND
THE NATIONAL GUIDED MISSILE
PROGRAM
1944-1950

By Max Rosenberg

**DEFENSE
LION**
PUBLICATIONS

Acknowledgements

This historical monograph was originally planned as part of a multi-volume history of the USAF guided missile program published by the USAF Historical Division Liaison Office. This work was never completed and the initial chapters were published as a monograph instead. This book is a compilation of that report with substantial additional material that updates and complements the original text.

Copyright Notice

CONTENTS

FOREWORD

This historical monograph was originally planned as part of a multi-volume history of the USAF guided missile program. However, personnel, organizational, and program realignments within the USAF Historical Division Liaison Office (AFCHO) forced abandonment of these plans. Consequently, the scope of the study is not that initially contemplated but its content seemed of sufficient interest to warrant publication.

The monograph covers generally the so-called national guided missile program that slowly evolved between the closing months of World War II and the beginning of the Korean War. More particularly, the monograph treats the interplay among the numerous national security agencies as it concerned guided missiles. The guided missile was among the first weapon systems to be subjected to the disadvantages as well as the advantages of constant scrutiny and intervention at the inter-service level. Moreover, this condition was aggravated no little by the interest, but not the forceful leadership, of a number of joint and other national security agencies a niche or more above the level of the services. In a sense, then, the guided missile became the 'guinea pig" from which grew the paradoxical situation of both a centralization and proliferation of authority and responsibility over weapon development and use. Only in recent years has this peculiar set of circumstances been altered under the persistent pressure of strong centralization the Office of the Secretary of Defense. For these reasons, the record of service actions and counteractions from the early guided missile years may well serve as a worthwhile addition to 'lessons learned' documentation.

JOSEPH W. ANGELL JR.

Chief, USAF Historical Division
Liaison Office

I. INTRODUCTION

"Modem science has utterly changed the nature of war and is still changing it," wrote Dr. Vannevar Bush, famed adviser on military research and development, in his 1949 treatise, Modem Arms and Free Man. In the years since these words were written, science has given warfare yet another new and fantastic dimension of destruction: guided missiles equipped with nuclear warheads capable of striking targets thousands of miles away.

Since the industrial revolution, modem scientific discoveries have had an increasingly important impact on human conflicts. The first World War wrought numerous scientific advances. World War II greatly accelerated them and helped mechanize warfare to a level previously unknown. Radar, jet-propelled aircraft, guided missiles, proximity fuses, and atom bombs were only a few of the new, spectacular products that played significant roles in the prosecution of the war.

The guided missile, like other instruments of war developed during World War II and subsequently refined, was stark evidence of mans relentless guest for improved weapons of destruction. Since first he threw stones at his adversaries, man had recognized the advantages of a missile-type weapon over hand-to-hand combat. In haphazard fashion he progressed from the use of the spear, sling, bow, catapult, and gun to the shell and bomb, always attempting to improve the speed, range, accuracy, and destructiveness of his "missiles."

Their effectiveness, however, left much to be desired; once released, a missile was subject to atmospheric elements, the miscalculations of its hurler, or the movements of its intended victim. With the advent of reaction propulsion and practical developments in the electromagnetic radiation and atomic energy fields, man at last possessed the means of overcoming these conditions. The era of guided missiles was at hand.

Definition of a Guided Missile

There are several definitions for the terms "missile" and "guided missile." The standard dictionary defines a missile as a weapon or object (spear, arrow, bullet, self-propelled rocket, or robot bomb) capable of being thrown, hurled, or projected to strike a distant object. It defines a guided missile more specifically as any missile whose course toward a target may be altered during passage by means of a self-contained mechanism controlled by radio signal, a built-in target-seeking radar or other devices. In a broader definition, the dictionary also includes missiles with preset controls, such as the German V-1 and V-2 or even underwater torpedoes. The USAF Dictionary accepts this broader description.

The definition settled upon by the military services in 1945 included any weapon intended to be projected, propelled, or flown to strike an object at a distance, the trajectory of which could be controlled by other than natural laws once it was fired. The Department of Defense's Research and Development

Board (RDB) changed this in 1948, limiting the designation to unmanned vehicles moving above the earth's surface whose flight path could be altered by a mechanism within the vehicle. The United States Air Force (USAF) still officially accepts the last definition.

Because of these variations in definition, application of the "guided missile" label to certain weapons has led to confusion and disagreement. Under the strictest interpretation, for example, none of the missiles employed operationally during World War II were really "guided missiles" since they failed to meet all criteria. A leading scientist, Dr. Clark B. Millikan, characterized the German V-l and V-2 with their preset controls as no more than "crude precursors".

German V-1 "Buzz Bomb" On Launch Catapult
Source: United States Army.

World War II guided glide and vertical bombs often fell within the "precursor" category also, since they lacked a mode of self-propulsion. Some observers contend that, since the guidance system receives and acts on information for only a few moments after launching, rocket-propelled missiles flying a ballistic trajectory fail to meet guided missile criteria and should be classified separately as ballistic missiles or ballistic rockets. Less commonly the term guided missile was reserved for winged, air-breathing vehicles. By and large, the services disregarded these distinctions and carried all of them in the guided missile category.

In the past, the distinction between a pilot-less aircraft and guided missile was of some significance. During World War II, the Army Air Force (AAF) regarded any unmanned vehicle with wings or other aerodynamic surfaces as pilot-less aircraft, not guided missiles. The Navy went further, formulating in

1945 an inter-bureau agreement on the two. Their separate and equal status was brief, and in 1946 pilot-less aircraft became a type or category within the guided missile family.

Beginning in 1951, the Air Force attempted to discourage use of the term guided missile by replacing it with the term pilot-less aircraft and employing aircraft nomenclature. Although the Air Force claimed that guided missiles were only an evolutionary extension of aircraft, the underlying purpose of the change was to discourage the other services from encroaching on Air Force missions and roles. In 1954, the Air Force reluctantly relinquished the terminology because of strong Army and Navy pressure.

Since about 1950, the Air Force has informally limited the guided missile designation to a vehicle meeting certain criteria -that it be unmanned, self-propelled, capable of accepting guidance information after launching, and contain a warhead. As always, there were several special-purpose exceptions: the reconnaissance and decoy missiles and those guided missiles modified as target drones. The nomenclature for the Matador tactical missile indicates the constant flux in terminology. Originally designated SSM-A-l, Matador became the B-61 in September 1951, then the TM-61 in November 1954 The target drone version became the QB-61.

Evolution of the Guided Missile

The idea of guiding a missile in flight had long occupied the minds of scientists, professional military men, and fiction writers. As early as the 1880s, Jules Verne featured a rocket-powered missile containing a target-seeker, a proximity fuse, and a warhead. In 1891, a respectable English engineering trade journal contained an advertisement alluding to a missile equipped with steam engine, propeller, wings, automatic controls, and warhead. Five years later, a British scientist, P. Y. Alexander, in his scholarly paper, "On Sounding the Air by Flying Machines Controlled by Hertzian Waves," proposed a supersonic vehicle under radio control.

Several nations experimented with guided missiles during World War I. In the United States, both the Army Air Service and the Navy built and flight tested versions with preset controls and reciprocating engines. England also experimented in this area, and in France, Pierre Lorin, who had designed a pulsejet power plant as early as 1907, proposed bombardment of Berlin by means of his "Torpille Aerienne". Powered by an aerothermal duct engine and fitted with a 440-pound warhead, the missile would be guided to its target by radio command from a "mother" aircraft. Lorin's efforts to interest the military authorities proved futile.

In the years between the two world wars, the military services and their scientific and industrial supporting agencies did little to develop guided missiles per se. But they made many advances in the state of the art and in the components--propulsion, electromagnetic, aerodynamic, etc. essential to a successful guided missile. By the outbreak of the second world conflict, a vast store of knowledge, many basic techniques, and some of the necessary components were at hand. The Allied nations chose not to exploit them, concentrating instead on the mass production of available weapons and modifying them as necessary. As a result, the Allied guided missile effort in World War II was limited basically to the addition of guidance or seeker devices to existing weapons.

The Germans, long restricted by the Versailles Treaty from the area of conventional ground and air weapons, turned their attention early to weapons outside the treaty provisions. The field of guided missiles constituted a likely avenue of pursuit, but the rate of progress was slow and the program suffered from inept high-level administration. By the time the Germans spectacularly unveiled their V-l and V-2 missiles, little doubt existed about the outcome of the war. Had they been equipped with atomic warheads, the missiles could have changed the whole complexion of the conflict. Lacking them and possessing relatively crude guidance equipment, the V-I and V-2 were no more than nuisance weapons and their immediate impact was primarily psychological.

German V-2 Rocket on Launch Trailer
Source: United States Air Force

When the U. S. exploded two atomic bombs over Japan in August 1945, it became obvious that, once perfected, the guided missile outfitted with an atomic warhead would force completely revised concepts of warfare.

AAF Guided Missiles Before and During World War II

As earlier indicated, guided missiles were of some interest to the Air Force (or more correctly, its predecessor organizations) during World War I. In 1917, under Army Signal Corps auspices, a group of engineering experts led by the renowned Charles F. Kettering began development of the "Bug" -- a miniature-sized airplane in which preset automatic controls replaced the pilot.

The Kettering Bug
Source: United States Army

The flight test program was sufficiently successful to prompt the Air Service to introduce the "Bug" into combat, but the war ended before production began. After the war, experiments with Bog variants continued for several years in somewhat desultory fashion. In 1928, the Army Air Corps discarded the specially built airframe in favor of a commercial airplane, to which it added remote control and guidance equipment.

The Depression caused discontinuance of this work in 1932. The Air Corps (The Army Air Service had become the Army Air Corps in July 1926) revived the experiments in 1938, at the direction of its Chief, Maj. Gen. Henry H. Arnold. After preparing a statement of military characteristics, the Experimental Engineering Section of the Materiel Division at Wright Field conducted a design competition but failed to elicit suitable proposals. General Arnold's continued interest caused the Air Corps to publish a revised statement of military characteristics in 1940 and to contract with General Motors Corporation in 1941 for development of 10 aerial torpedoes (subsequently redesignated power-driven controllable bombs) plus control and launching equipment. The missile would be capable of hitting a 200-foot target at a range of 20 miles. This was the first of many guided missile contracts that the AAF let immediately before and during World War II. Although the wartime missile development program appeared extensive, it actually was nothing more than a hodgepodge of about 60 projects divided into three broad groups: flying bombs, glide bombs, and vertical bombs. None proved to be of real importance in winning the war.

The AAF classified missiles containing a propulsion unit and some type of remote or automatic control as power-driven, controllable bombs or flying bombs. General Motors A-1, first of this group, underwent extensive flight testing during 1941 and 1942, Because control system difficulties indicated the need of a long period of development, the AAF dropped the project in August 1943 in favor of several other flying bomb experiments. These were the BQ-series of remotely controlled conventional and target airplanes. Work on six different models was expensive and slow, officials soon questioned their tactical worth, and they too were dropped.

Beginning early in 1944, the AAF began converting obsolescent war-weary aircraft to flying bombs. During the next two years, it experimented with B-17, B-24, P-38, P-47, P-63, and other aircraft in combination with numerous types of radio, television (TV), and radar guidance equipment and several different homing devices. Flights of several B-17Fs against German targets proved largely unsuccessful. Faced with unreliable radio, TV, and radar control equipment, experimental seeker devices, and unsatisfactory war-weary aircraft performance, the AAF diverted its effort from these flying bombs.

Intelligence reports and then operational flights of the German V-1 buzz bomb, beginning in June 1944, provided impetus for the AAF to develop jet-propelled flying bombs. using parts from expended V-1s, Wright Field and Republic Aviation engineers quickly reconstructed the pulsejet propulsion unit and then the entire missile. By 8 September 1944, they had assembled the first complete JB-2, a Chinese copy of the V-1, and in October began test launchings at Eglin Field, Florida. Grandiose AAF production plans would have permitted 500 JB-2 sorties per day, but the War Department General Staff rejected the proposal on logistic and strategic grounds. The AAF then reduced its requirements to less than seven percent of the original proposal. After V-E Day, the General staff imposed another drastic reduction, and, in September 1945 the AAF terminated all contracts. Altogether, contractors produced 1,391 JB-2s.

The JB-2 Missile
Source: United States Army

The AAF encountered major difficulty in developing a completely satisfactory JB-2 launching technique, although experimenting with concrete ramps, B-17s, and Navy escort aircraft carriers (CVE). Nor were AAF experiments to obtain increased range and accuracy particularly successful. After determining that technical and tactical considerations did not warrant continued development, the AAF closed out the JB-2 project in March 1946.

The AAF had several other jet-propelled flying bomb projects, but only two progressed beyond the study stage. The first was Northrop Aircraft's JB-I (and a modified version the JB-10). Built in a flying wing configuration and powered by a General Electric turbojet and later by an Americanized version of the V-1 pulsejet, the JB-1 and JB-10 displayed numerous shortcomings in a series of test flights starting in December 1944. Since only a costly and extended development period could eliminate deficiencies, the AAF in March 1946 ended the project. Hughes Aircraft's JB-3 Tiamat was the other jet-propelled flying bomb. Built in cooperation with National Advisory Committee for Aeronautics (NACA) as a research vehicle, the JB-3 was used by Hughes for that purpose in its postwar air-to-air missile investigations.

Work on the second group of missiles -- glide bombs and torpedoes -- began early in 1941 and continued in haphazard fashion throughout the war. The glide bomb, a standard bomb with an attached winged structure and control or bombing device, possessed no propulsive unit and was carried externally by a bomber which served as its launching platform. Altogether, the AAF developed 15 differently designated glide bombs and one glide torpedo. They differed from one another in the type of control or homing device employed. Three versions -- the GB-l, GB-4, and GT-l underwent combat service testing but were found wanting in many respects.

It was only with the third group of guided missiles, controllable vertical bombs, that the AAF enjoyed limited success, and only this part of the wartime program was retained once hostilities ceased. These were standard free-fall bombs fitted with a tail containing control surfaces and stabilizing devices. At first, the bombardier visually controlled the azimuth of the falling bomb by radio signal. Later improvements allowed control of both azimuth and range. In other experiments, the AAF studied the use of TV and of heat, light, and radar seekers for controlling the bombs fall.

Thirteen of these vertical bombs received separate VB-designations but only the first, the VB-I or Azon (azimuth only) saw combat in World War II. Employed against railroads, bridges, and tunnels in Italy and France, Azon revealed wide dispersion patterns and required extended runs over the target by its director airplane. Following modification, Azon achieved better results in the India-Burma theater.

The AAF could find little satisfaction with its World War II guided missile program largely because its scope had been limited to so-called short-term development. Perhaps as great a handicap was the initial lack of any central direction over the program. Arnold initially assigned overall management authority within the Air Staff to the Air Communications Office while development responsibility at Wright Field went to the Equipment Laboratory. Not until late in the war were functions shifted to normal channels of command and organization. The program also lacked adequate financial support, technically qualified personnel, and satisfactory facilities, and it was not until the V-l and V-2 launchings that guided missiles received more than casual attention from top AAF officials.

This top-level attention involved political considerations almost as much as technical and operational requirements. The AAF pushed JB-2 development and operational use despite protests that the cost was not worth the effort and that the European tactical situation did not require missiles. Undaunted when plans were overtaken by events, in Europe, the AAF sought to use the JB-2 in the Pacific area, only to be overtaken again. By using the JB-2 in combat, the AAF had hoped to enhance its prestige and its claims to overall guided missile responsibility. Even before the end of the war, the three major Army elements – the AAF, the Army Ground Forces (AGF), and the Army Service Forces (ASF) -- had begun maneuvering to obtain a share of the larger prize: retention or acquisition of roles in the postwar missions of air defense, tactical support, and strategic bombardment.[1]

II. THE SERVICE CONTEST FOR MISSILE RESPONSIBILITIES

Through 1943, only the Army Air Force (AAF) of the Army's three major forces displayed any interest in guided missiles. The advent of the German V-1 and V-2, however, stirred the AAF, Army Ground Forces (AGF), and Army Service Forces (ASF) into hurried action to obtain sophisticated self-propelled and guided missiles. Realizing the potential of the guided missile, they also began maneuvering to gain major responsibility for development and operational control.

The nature of a guided missile provided no clear basis for making decisions. The AAF claimed that the missile was no more than an advance in aircraft technology, with control and guidance equipment replacing the pilot. The AGF and ASF contended that the guided missile was only an evolutionary extension of artillery. These points of view were, of course, specious and quite academic, for the crux of the arguments lay elsewhere. At stake was the preservation or enlargement of the missions and roles of the three Army forces. The AAF wanted to keep its air defense, close air support, and strategic bombardment roles and obtain AGF's antiaircraft artillery functions The AGF, on the other hand, wanted a part of the AAF mission and control of guided missiles appeared a means to this end.

There were a number of other factors not directly concerned with guided missiles that affected postwar missile planning. Late in the war, Arnold had predicted that advances in guided missiles and atomic energy would cause revised concepts of warfare and that AAF's future existence would depend on measures taken to obtain these advances. A small band of enthusiasts within the Air Staff and elsewhere in the AAF agreed with Arnold and attempted to take action. Others, usually in the more influential positions, acknowledged the potential of guided missiles but felt that their importance was some years away and that more immediate organizational, technological, and financial problems required solution.

To the AAF, the most important of these problems was independence. Air partisans had gradually diminished the hold of the ground and service forces over the air arm and had finally gained a large measure of autonomy in 1942. AAF officials made complete independence their first order of business after the war. Any matter that could jeopardize these negotiations at the War Department, Presidential, and congressional levels were set aside or handled with circumspection. As a consequence, the AAF frequently took less vigorous stands in the discussions on assigning guided missile development and operational responsibilities than it might otherwise have done.

The technological advances during the last years of World War II also diverted AAF interest from the guided missile. The most important of these were the jet-propelled airplane and the atomic bomb. Guaranteed a long period of peace, the AAF might have relied on using available weapons while awaiting perfection of nuclear-armed guided missiles. But even before the war ended, Soviet Union intransigence had alerted the Western nations to maintain a semblance of military readiness. In the wake of hasty demobilization, the atom bomb constituted the main source of American military power and the airplane the only readily available means of delivering the bomb. With little real choice in the matter, AAF officials emphasized development of modem jet aircraft at the expense of the still unproven guided missile. In the light of their lower priority, guided missiles stood no chance of obtaining an adequate share of the drastically reduced postwar military appropriations, and the AAF's initial comprehensive development plan was soon emasculated beyond recognition.

Some critics have alleged that AAI. military leaders—virtually all pilots -- relied on the airplane in the postwar period in a manner reminiscent of Army generals who refused to give up the cavalry and admirals who wished to retain the battleship. While there were those who manifested such an attitude, it was primarily a combination of circumstances and prudence that led the AAF to rely so heavily on its proven weapon system--the airplane -- immediately after the war.

Against dire warnings by a few that failure to expedite development of the guided missile would leave the Air Force technologically outmoded and possibly deprived of essential roles and missions, responsible AAF leaders were forced to weigh the realities of new military crises, the need to deal with sudden conflict, and limited funds to maintain a force-in-being. With victory there also emerged a new emphasis on air power. In view of these realities and the time and cost required to develop infinitely more complex guided missiles, it was not surprising that the Air Force gave development precedence to the airplane.

Emergence of the Intra-service Missile Controversy

As indicated above, conflicting views on the antecedents of the guided missile and its proper role in supporting assigned service missions and functions soon had the three Army forces at odds. Initially, the AAF-ASF dispute over development was the more acute. However, since the combat forces prepared statements of military characteristics on the basis of their requirements and conducted training and operational planning in advance of weapon availability, the AAF and AGF were soon joined over the question of operational responsibility.

AGF-ASF interest in guided missiles greatly intensified in 1944, after receipt of intelligence reports on German developments and subsequent employment of the V-1 and V-2. In February 1944, AGF asked ASF to develop an antiaircraft guided rocket; in July, AGF broadened its requirements to include a family of guided missiles to replace conventional field artillery. About the same time, Gen. George C. Marshall, Army Chief of Staff, had indicated his intention to assign all guided missile development responsibility to the AAF. However, AGF's latest request to ASF (the Ordnance Department in particular) and Navy complaints about inter-service confusion and lack of adequate coordination caused several top War Department officials to re-examine the subject of missiles. [1]

On 2 August 1944, Robert A. Lovett, Assistant Secretary of War for Air, observed that AGF wanted a duplicate of the V-1, which the AAF already had under construction as the JB-2. He suggested that General Arnold and his AGF counterpart decide where the weapon belonged.

Robert A. Lovett
Source: U.S. DoD

Lovett personally believed that responsibility should be left with the AAF, since the JB-2 basic configuration and control system were most akin to aircraft. General Arnold asked Maj. Gen. Harold A. Craig, his Assistant Chief of Air Staff for Operations, Commitments, and Requirements (AC/AS, OC&R), to investigate. Craig then sought the assistance of Edward L. Bowles, expert consultant to both the Secretary of War and Arnold, who concluded that no duplication existed in the development area between the AAF and Ordnance Department (ASF) and that division of work on AGF requirements between the two agencies would be quite simple. Craig emphasized these views in his reply to Arnold. [2]

On 17 August, Arnold reported to Lovett that "there appears to be ample room in the rocket field for both Air and Ground Forces." He foresaw no difficulty over the assignment of pilot-less aircraft, as distinct from wingless rockets, but observed that the JB-2 should be placed in combat, needed or not, as an insurance measure for AAF claims. [3]

Some Air Staff members believed that this oversimplified an issue that was more than one of winged versus wingless missiles or of technical duplication and competition. They feared that the AGF-ASF program, even if restricted to wingless missiles, would thwart AAF plans to gain control of the antiaircraft artillery function (currently under AGF jurisdiction). More importantly, it might endanger the AAF's air defense, close air support, and strategic bombardment roles. [4]

Even before Arnold had reported his findings to Lovett, Col. Roscoe C. Wilson of the Air Staff's Development Engineering Branch in a move to forestall independent ASF activity had asked the Materiel Command at Wright Field to prepare plans for conducting a missile development program in cooperation with ASF agencies. Asserting that the AGF-stated military characteristics of 22 July duplicated those earlier formulated in the Air Staff, he warned that development of both sets of weapons would result in competition and priority squabbles for scientific personnel, equipment, and facilities. As expected, the Materiel Command proposed to concentrate guided missile development under its jurisdiction, with the ASF technical services assisting as necessary. [5]

By September 1944, enough high Air Staff members had become sufficiently concerned over the possible effects of the AGE-ASF missile program on AAF roles and missions to draft a proposal placing all missile development under the AAF.. Under the War Department reorganization directive of 2 March 1942, ASF was responsible for developing and procuring all materiel required by the ground and air forces except equipment peculiar to the AAF. They reasoned that guided missiles fell into this excepted category because the AAF possessed appropriate development and production facilities and the end product would resemble an aircraft or use control equipment peculiar to it. On this premise, development and procurement functions were logically AAF responsibilities if the missile met any of the following criteria: essentially an aircraft; capable of sustained aerodynamic flight; launched or controlled from an airplane controlled by a device assigned, to or employed by the AAF; used against an aerial target; used as an alternative or additional bombing weapon or supplemented fighter aircraft.

The proposal that Lt. Gen. Barney M. Giles, Chief of Air Staff, dispatched to the War Department on 7 September 1944 was far less emphatic and detailed. contending only that "guided missiles generally fall within the developmental jurisdiction of the Army Air Forces," Giles asked for authority to direct development of all guided missiles "including any joint developments". At the same time, he proposed to the Ordnance Department that it participate in a joint program under AAF direction to avoid unnecessary duplication and competition.

The McNarney Directive

By this time the War Department General Staff (WDGS) had become deeply involved in the service jurisdictional issues. Here, AGF and ASF were assured of a friendly audience for their point of view. After lengthy discussions with representatives from the Joint Chiefs of Staff (JCS) and the three Army forces, the WDGS New Developments Division on 14 September 1944 drafted a policy for allocating development responsibilities within the guided missile field. In forwarding the proposal., Brig. Gen. William A. Borden, the division's director (and an Ordnance officer), explained that until recently guided bombs, torpedoes, and war-weary aircraft had constituted the major part of the guided missile effort. For this reason, General Marshall had intended to assign all development responsibility to the AAF. There was now a growing interest in "long range" (self-propelled) missiles, both of the flying (winged) and rocket (wingless) types, for use against zone-of-communication and strategic targets. Since state of the art on these missiles was not yet sufficiently advanced, WDGS could not realistically evaluate requirements or assign operational control to one of the two combat forces. On the other hand, there was definite need for a coordinated and orderly research and development program.

The Army Deputy Chief of Staff, Lt. Gen. Joseph T. McNarney (an AAF officer), approved the policy statement (soon known as the McNarney Directive) on 2 October 1944. Under its provisions, the AAF received development responsibility for guided missiles launched from aircraft and for surface-launched missiles which depended primarily on aerodynamic lift for sustaining flight. The ASF (Ordnance Department) would develop surface-launched missiles that depended primarily on momentum for flight sustenance. Development of integral missile components (propulsion and control subsystems) fell within the purview of the missile-developing agency. In contrast, this agency would use the

Lt. Gen. J. T. McNarney
Source: U.S.A.F.

ASF technical services to develop warheads, non-integral launching devices, and ground portions of the control system. For the time being, AGF could prepare statements of military characteristics in accordance with what it deemed its requirements and then ask the AAF or ASF to develop the missile. The AAF could also prepare statements and either undertake the development work or ask ASF to do it. The three forces were to coordinate their efforts fully and exchange information freely so that as a missile neared operational status, the AAF and AGF could evaluate its potentialities against their needs. Until missiles approached this point, the Chief of Staff would make no exclusive operational assignments.

The McNarney Directive constituted the sole policy guidance on guided missiles within the Army for the next two years, even though it had a number of major faults. The directive was a compromise. It divided the guided missile field on a technological basis that was both unrealistic and untenable. Moreover, the directive was vaguely written, leading to widely divergent interpretations of its provisions. Finally, it avoided the operational responsibility issue. As a consequence, the three Army forces soon put the policy under attack, directly by the AAF and more covertly by the other two.

The AAF Drive to Revise the McNarney Directive

The AAF initially attacked the McNarney Directive because it failed to settle the question of operational responsibility. The AAF did this with two objectives in mind: to gain the lions share of the operational assignments while restricting the role of the AGF and then win by default responsibility for research, development, procurement, and training. As a first step, the AAF used a missile almost ready for combat. By late 1944, the JB-2 had approached production status and both the AAF and AGF stated operational requirements for its use and planned to form and train JB-2 combat units. On 1 January 1945, the New Developments Division informed Lt. Gen. Thomas T. Handy, McNarney's successor as Army Deputy Chief of Staff, about the JB-2 controversy and asked for a ruling. General Marshall immediately decided verbally in favor of the AAF.

The Air Staff wanted to strike for operational control of all missiles for which the AAF had development responsibility, justifying the step on the basis "that the future of the AAF lies to a great extent with pilot-less and guided or controlled missiles" and that the confusion resulting from the McNarney Directive endangered that future. Although several top Air Staff members labeled the resulting proposal as "hot" and of "far-reaching implications", General Giles submitted to WDGS only a request for written confirmation of Marshall's verbal decision on the JB-2 "and similar type guided missiles"

The WDGS Operations Division (OPD) quickly confirmed the specific JB-2 assignment but added that the question of operational responsibility for all guided missiles was under study. On the following day, OPD asked the WDGS organization and Training Division (G-3) to study the subject and recommend revisions to the McNarney Directive.

Upon receipt of this news, Giles forwarded on 6 February the draft policy proposal earlier prepared by the Air staff. In forwarding it, Giles explained that operational assignments were necessary now to avoid duplication or inadequate operational planning. Realistic allocations could only be made in terms of service missions and the technical characteristics of each missile. The AAF proposal contained two slight but subtle changes to the McNarney Directive. While ASF would still develop momentum (or ballistic) missiles, the AAF would develop all guided missiles whose flight sustenance depended primarily on forces other than momentum.

The second change involved AGF's rights to prepare statements of military characteristics for and to use any surface-launched missile. Under the AAF proposal, these rights would be limited to missiles which replaced artillery or close support aircraft in the immediate ground battle and ballistic missiles which replaced anti-aircraft artillery. This meant that the AAF could prepare military characteristics statements and use all air-launched-missiles, all missiles used against targets to the rear of the immediate ground battle, and all interceptor missiles other than wingless. The ASF and AAF would still depend on the technical services to develop missile components.

The AAF proposal took about five weeks to get from OPD to G-3, "conveniently" arriving there on 17 March 1945, just after G- 3 had completed its own plan. G-3 promised to study the AAF plan after the three Army forces had commented on its own proposal. The division proposed no change to the McNarney Directive and discussed only the issue of operational assignments. Although believing that it was premature to make final operational assignments, the division thought that interim assignments were in order to keep the guided missile program within reasonable bounds.

G-3 quickly disposed of air-launched missiles, recommending that they be assigned to the AAF. In the field of surface-launched missiles, G-3 suggested the following operational line-up: those used for strategic bombardment, fighter sweep, escort, distant interception, and sea-target bombardment missions should be assigned to the AAF; those employed in lieu of field and seacoast artillery should be assigned to the AGF; finally, missiles used for tactical bombardment and "point" air defense purposes should be available to both forces. since AAF and AGF might require the same missile at a time when its availability was limited, the Chief of Staff would make a decision as the need arose.[16]

The Air Staff reluctantly concurred with G- 3 but pointed to its 6 February proposal as a "clearer and more definite" policy to prevent duplication of weapons and unite and promote economy of forces. The AGF opposed the G-3 proposal on the grounds that all surface-launched missiles belonged under its control, and the powerful OPD tended to support this position. When G-3 issued a slightly revised draft in May 1945, the Air Staff reluctantly agreed to its terms after reiterating the view that the AAF version was more desirable. Air Staff members explained their quick acceptance on the basis of political expediency. In their words, "the ramifications incident to establishment of a permanent policy render an interim solution more desirable and provide more flexibility when the Air Force assumes its increased. stature in a Department of National Defense and the proposal represented as great a concession as the AAF are likely to obtain at this time."

On 21 June 1945, Brig. Gen. Henry I. Hodes, Army Assistant Deputy Chief of Staff, announced that Marshall had disapproved the proposal and that the McNarney Directive would remain unchanged. Hodes explained that "the development, characteristics, control and capabilities of these missiles have not developed to the point where definite assignment of the operational employment to a major command can be determined without the possibility of jeopardizing future development." The Chief of Staff, he added, would make such assignments only after a missile had reached the point where its actual characteristics and capabilities had been compared against the mission requirements of the combat forces. [18]

Brig. Gen. Henry I. Hodes
Source: USAF

The rejection surprised the Air Staff, and some members wanted Arnold to appeal directly to Marshall in behalf of the AAF's 6 February proposal. Other staff officials foresaw little chance of its acceptance and thought the appeal would likely prejudice the AAF position at a later date. Hode's decision, commented one officer, appeared "wholely [sic] reasonable" and did not conflict with AAF interests. There was no denying that missile characteristics and capabilities were still unknown; asking Marshall to make operational assignments at this time was, in reality, asking him "to buy a pig in a poke and he might even end up by thinking (as I do) that we are evidencing more interest in the assignment of guided missiles than in their development and use."[19]

Brig. Gen. William F. McKee, Deputy AC/AEOC&R, told his immediate superior, Lt. Gen. Hoyt S. Vandenberg, that the objections were indeed valid and that "perhaps we would do better by getting our own house in order, place more concentrated energy and emphasis on the guided missiles program for the Air Forces and then fighting for what we think is right."

Because this was a policy matter with far reaching implications, McKee suggested that Vandenberg discuss the subject further with Gen. Ira C. Eaker, AAF Deputy commander, and other top staff officials. In the end, the AAF deferred its appeal; in assigning the papers to the files, an officer cautioned prophetically: "it is absolutely certain that sooner or later we will have to write some high-powered letters on the subject."

Brig. Gen. William F. McKee
Source: USAF

Continued Dissatisfaction With the McNarney Directive

The six-month foray to rescind the McNarney Directive and obtain operational assignments had come to naught. Interest disappeared at the top levels of the Air Staff although not in the lower echelons. In July and August 1945, they learned that ASF (Ordnance Department) intended to make its Nike antiaircraft missile maneuverable in flight – in short, from the AAF point of view, to have it act as an interceptor aircraft by adding airfoils. Moreover, ASF planned to extend the range of its Ordcit surface-to-surface missiles by the addition of what AAF personnel deemed to be wings; the ASF called them fins.

AAF missile officials regarded these ASF actions as an invasion of their development province. They resented the fact that ASF had bypassed the AAF and gone directly to Douglas Aircraft Company for assistance with the airfoils and wings in apparent violation of the McNarney Directive. Still another source of discontent was a Signal Corps effort to develop a missile detection, warning, and control system that, in the opinion of AAF officers, clearly belonged to the AAF under an October 1944 agreement transferring responsibility for certain classes of electronic materiel from the Signal Corps to the AAF.

A report of these grievances and a proposed statement of policy (restricting ASF to the development of wingless, surface-to-surface missiles) was drawn up in the Air Staff working level. Although the Air Staff agreed with their substance, it decided that the time was not propitious for action, undoubtedly because of the pending postwar War Department Reorganization then under study. [21]

Late in November 1945, Maj. Gen. Lauris Norstad, AC/AS-5, furnished new impetus for reopening the missile question by issuing a policy guidance statement on "future" AAF functions and responsibilities which encouraged interpretation of them "in their broadest aspects." The AAF was the nation's primary defense force and had to be capable of repelling all attacks -- land, sea, and air. Therefore, it should obtain any superior weapon aerodynamically sustained or self-propelled in flight and "we should recognize no limitations -- geographical, functional or technical -- upon the employment of these weapons." Norstad admitted that there were no specific agreements on exact functions and responsibilities for the Army forces and the Navy; nevertheless, "in planning future strategy, in procuring and developing new weapons, in training future air force unite, and in coordinating projected operations, the Army Air Forces should not limit their [sic] outlook to any restricted responsibility. [22]

Maj. Gen. Lauris Norstad
Source: U.S.A.A.F

This broad guidance coming at a time when working-level personnel were still dissatisfied with the War Department's missile policies caused them to press again for a favorable resolution. At their request, AC/AS-5's Policy Division called a meeting on 6 December 1945, at which Air Staff representatives agreed to prepare an all-inclusive study for submission to the new Army Chief of Staff, Gen. Dwight D. Eisenhower. [23] (Eisenhower became Chief of Staff on 19 Nov 1945 and served until 7 Feb 1948.)

While work on the study was still in progress, General Eaker was briefed on 2 January 1946 by his executive officer, Col. Turner A. Sims, on the current uncertainties in the missile program and the widespread fears that the AAF might lose portions of its mission so long as these uncertainties remained. The next day, Eaker discussed the matter at the regular meeting of the Air Staff, and Gen. Carl Spaatz, Chief of Air Staff, then introduced the idea of having ASF develop non-guided or non-controlled missiles while the AAF developed those controllable after launching. The Air Staff agreed with this approach, but felt it should not be submitted to WDGS until the AAF had carried out and publicized, a 1, 000-mile Banshee flight, currently scheduled for August 1946. (Project Banshee, the modification of a B-29 to an unmanned configuration, proved a failure).

Gen. Carl Spaatz
Source: U.S.A.A.F.

Spaatz posed the missile issue in passing, however, early in January 1946. While expounding to Eisenhower his views on the AAF mission, Spaatz listed such responsibilities as air defense of the United States and its possessions, establishment and operation of air warning systems, and research, development, and procurement of missiles controlled or guided after launching. On 26 January 1946, Eisenhower informally agreed in principle, but pointed out that AGF and Navy also had air defense responsibilities. Although he acknowledged the lack of missile operational assignments, Eisenhower added that they should await further advances in development. [25] An Air Staff member later commented that General Borden had probably prepared the Chief of Staff's reply and that it indicated continuance of the status quo.

Re-examination of the McNarney Directive

Much to the gratification of the AAF, the General Staff on 13 February 1946 reopened the subject of development assignments. Perhaps this was a result of the Spaatz-Eisenhower exchange, studies then under way in JCS, or industry complaints of blatant duplication. Eisenhower asked the AAF, AGF, and ASF to review the McNarney Directive and suggest modifications to cover assignments among the three Army forces.

On 4 March, General Spaatz, who succeeded Arnold as the AAF's commanding general on 1 March, replied for the AAF. Although he believed that there was little undesirable duplication in the AAF and ASF missile programs, Spaatz feared that as research and study narrowed the paths of development, duplication and competition for limited funds, facilities, and scientific personnel would undoubtedly result. Spaatz outlined four possible solutions:

- retain the McNarney Directive with re-emphasis on interagency cooperation, pending further development progress;

- retain the current directive unchanged but rely more heavily on the technical services to develop missile components;

- arbitrarily allocate development responsibilities between the AAF and ASF on the basis of missile range or operational use;

- assign development of all guided missiles controllable in flight to the AAF.

Spaatz voiced strong opposition to establishment of a central War Department coordinating office, like the Navy's, to approve and place projects with the forces. Such an office, he declared, would be a "bottleneck", require a vast expansion of the New Developments Division, and could operate only under extremely formal procedures.

Spaatz argued that centralization of development under the AAF provided the best safeguards against duplication. Other benefits would accrue from relying upon the proper Army technical agency to develop components. And since missiles with a range beyond that of current artillery projectiles required guidance in flight, use of AAF-developed aeronautical components was essential. Should the General Staff not agree, Spaatz recommended continuance of the status quo with reliance on the technical services to develop major missile components. [27]

Not unexpectedly, other War Department agencies turned down the AAF proposal. In turn, the AAF disagreed on a revised version of the McNarney Directive proposed by the New Developments Division because it did not clearly define lines of development responsibility between the AAF and ASF and so failed to accomplish its avowed purpose. At the suggestion of Maj. Gen. Curtis E. LeMay, AAF Deputy Chief of Staff for Research and Development, representatives from WDGS, AAF,

Gen Curtis E LeMay
Source: U.S.A.F.

AGF, and ASF met on 25 March 1946, but were unable to resolve the basic AAF - ASF differences. The ASF refused to relinquish the right to develop maneuverable-in-flight missiles; the AAF would not concede ASF's right to develop such missiles because they required autopilots, remote control devices, and airfoils -- all items under AAF development and procurement cognizance.

Perturbed by the outcome of these discussions and fearful that continued disagreement within the War Department might result in Navy seizure of guided missile development, several Air Staff members the next day drew up a new draft policy statement and proposed that Spaatz discuss it with Eisenhower. Under its terms, the AAF would prepare military characteristics for air -launched and those surface-launched guided missiles used in strategic and air defense missions. The AGF would do the same for close support and self-propelled but unguided air defense missiles. In the development area, the AAF would build all controllable-in-flight missiles and ASF all unguided missiles (a shift from the aerodynamic-versus-momentum division). Both would use the technical capabilities of the other and encourage joint contracting. Before either began development, the New Developments Division would review project objectives for duplication. The AAF proposal also contained one major operational concession -- the right of AGF to exercise sole control over close support missiles -- but it would be excluded from using guided air defense missiles.

Spaatz initially decided to use the draft as an internal policy statement "to govern our staff thinking and future planning on this subject." Then, on 29 April 1946, he sent the proposal to General Handy for WDGS consideration, There was no immediate reaction from the General Staff, due primarily to the imminent War Department reorganization. Eisenhower explained that he wanted General Borden's successor at that time to review missile policies and recommend revisions.

Maj. Gen. Henry S. Aurand
Source: U.S. Army

The reorganization, directed on 14 May 1946, became effective on 11 June. ASF was eliminated and its former units, although independent of each other, were collectively called the Technical Services. Maj. Gen. Henry S. Aurand (an Ordnance officer) became WDGS Director of Research and Development. His AAF counterpart, General LeMay, instructed the Air Staff to acquaint Aurand fully with all AAF development projects, particularly those for guided missiles. These instructions were more than adequately carried out through means of a special briefing on 12 July and by Aurand's two-day (18 to 19 July) visit to Wright Field. [30]

These special measures seemed to no avail. In a series of meetings during August -September 1946, the WDGS, AAF and Technical Services sought a satisfactory solution to the missile development impasse, and it appeared that the AAF might well be fighting a hopeless battle. According to AAF representatives, Aurand had expressed the view that the AAF program was too large, contained much duplication, and had insufficient talent to carry it out. He also claimed that guided missiles were basically rockets, not pilot-less aircraft, and that their development was closely allied to rockets. And AAF interest in missiles was questionable since it dealt with pilots. [31]

Aurand incorporated much of these views in a proposal late in September 1946. The AAF quickly rejected the plan because it would result in shifting most AAF missile projects to the Ordnance Department while keeping development responsibilities divided. In his report to Spaatz on the proposal, LeMay emphasized that "the long-range future of the AAF lies in the field of guided missiles" and the AAF must "stick to its guns". He added that the AAF proposal of last April was the only satisfactory basis for discussion; during the five months that had elapsed no one had formally refuted its facts and logic. [32]

Rescission of the McNarney Directive

In the fall of 1946, other top civilian and military officials of the War Department entered the missile controversy and swiftly moved it to a conclusion. The immediate cause for their participation was the rising number of complaints from scientific and industrial leaders that military agencies were frequently asking for duplicating research and development, thereby wasting money, personnel, and facilities.

W. Stuart Symington, Assistant Secretary of State for Air, and Generals Spaatz and Handy Joined the previous participants to eliminate the condition and prevent recurrence. They narrowed their solutions down to one of several possibilities:

- establish a separate development task force independent of both the AAF and the Ordnance Department;

- assign development operating control to Aurand's Research and Development Division at the General Staff level;

- assign the entire guided missile development program to an existing agency.

The consensus was that the last possibility was the most attractive and that the AAF was the most logical and best equipped agency to operate the program. [33]

Maj. Gen. Everett S. Hughes, Chief of Ordnance, under considerable pressure, reluctantly agreed but only after gaining the concession that his department would retain development of some "guided objects or projectiles". Other Army officers feared that the AAF would quite naturally give priority to its own developments, neglecting AGF requirements, and that limited funding would aggravate this tendency. To minimize this danger, the conferees agreed that the General Staff Director of Research and Development should referee all disputes. [34]

Shortly before the end of September, Aurand forwarded a draft statement, announcing the results. LeMay quickly dissented because the statement was both policy and implementative in nature, containing decisions on matters which Aurand, as the War Department final arbiter, should not have made until the development agencies reported their inability to agree. Suggesting that the policy statement be clear cut and concise, LeMay drafted a substitute, stating that the AAF was responsible for the Army guided missile (and countermeasures) development program but would make maximum use of scientific talent and facilities of other Army units. A technical committee with representatives from these units would assist in deciding to start, revise, or discontinue projects." [35]

Stuart Symington
Source: U.S. Air Force

Aurand accepted LeMay's version with one change. Possibly to safeguard Ordnance Department and Signal Corps interests more fully, he deleted reference to the technical committee and stated that the Director of Research and Development would determine which of the current (and future) projects belonged in the guided missile field. After Secretary of War Robert P. Patterson approved the revised policy statement, General Hodes issued it on 7 October 1946. [36]

After more than two years, the AAF had finally won rescission of the McNarney Directive. Mr. Symington, in an 8 October press conference, described the new directive as possibly the most important national defense decision ever made, for it would prevent the waste of millions of dollars in duplicating effort. He also used the opportunity to make a "sales pitch" for unification, declaring that the directive went only part of the way in eliminating wasteful duplication and urging creation of a single defense department to complete the job. [37]

AAF Assumption of Development Management

On 10 October 1946, Aurand notified the Ordnance Department and Signal Corps that they would continue their current development projects under the cognizance of the AAF but with no transfer of funds, personnel, contracts, and facilities "at this time." The two technical services would review their work by 22 October and determine what part fell into the guided missile field and should be under AAF cognizance. The AAF would examine the War Department program and prepare a plan for its administration. Following some acrimonious interagency discussion over what work rightfully belonged in the missile area, Aurand on 26 November 1946 approved the AAF plan of management. [38]

The plan called for continuance of the current program until the AAF Technical Committee, a recently established group to oversee all AAF research and development work (not guided missiles alone), had analyzed all projects and decided whether to continue, cancel, or consolidate them. In requesting new missile projects, the AAF or AGF would prepare statements of military characteristics and send them to the AAF through the War Department General Staff. The AAF Technical Committee would then establish all priorities, determine the proper agency to undertake development, pass on contracts, and, beginning in fiscal year 1949, coordinate the missile budgetary requests of the Technical Services. The developing agency would conduct acceptance tests and procure service-test missiles. In any instance of disagreement, the WDGS Director of Research and Development would make final ruling. [39]

This system of management continued until March 1948, some six months after the establishment of the United States Air Force (USAF). Considering the bitterness which preceded its creation, the system worked reasonably well. The participants seldom called on the referee. Only once did the AAF Technical Committee complain officially of lack of cooperation by the Technical Services. The system furnished a common platform for discussion and encouraged interagency planning. Only one point of contact between the Army and industry eased the problem of blatant technical duplication, especially in the subsystem and component area. And the system facilitated the exchange of technical information among the interested agencies. [40]

The 7 October policy directive and the subsequent implementing orders had provided the AAF with little of its long-sought objectives. The Ordnance Department still had authority to develop guided missiles. It concentrated on surface-to-surface and surface-to-air ballistic rockets, but could now employ essential airfoils without fear of violating the terms of the rescinded McNarney Directive. The AAF enjoyed the prerogative of "looking over Ordnance's shoulder" and of exerting pressure when duplication of effort appeared. But should a technical committee decision be distasteful, Ordnance could appeal to a most receptive audience and sympathetic arbiter in the General Staff.

Operational Responsibility Unresolved

While the War Department worked out a compromise on development responsibility, the vexing question of AAF and AGF operational control over surface-launched guided missiles, unsettled but dormant since mid-1945, arose again. On 26 August 1946 and again on 15 October, the AGF requested the Chief of Staff for the operational control of all surface-launched missiles. Asked by the General Staff for its views, the AAF suggested that short-range or close-support surface-to-surface missiles be assigned to the AGF and the remainder (long-range surface-to-surface, surface-to-air, air-to-air, and air-to-surface) to the AAF.

WDGS took little additional action on the matter, although the AGF in mid-January 1947 again prodded for a decision. [41]

Operational control of the surface-to-air missile was a persistent topic in 1946, being largely the by-product of AAF-AGF long-time contentions over the air defense mission. The AAF claimed the mission as one of its major responsibilities and wanted control over all air defense forces and weapons. The AGF regarded air defense as no more than a portion of its task of defending the continental United States (CONUS) from attack. Interwoven into this major problem were two other issues: control of antiaircraft artillery weapons currently assigned to the AGF and claimed by the AAF and of surface-to-air guided missiles which the AGF deemed to be only an extension of antiaircraft artillery, a stand the AAF. heatedly denied. [42]

Early postwar proposals and counterproposals had not produced a solution to these problems. However, on 14 May 1946, the Secretary of War directed a tentative readjustment of organization and functional assignments within the War Department, subject to final revision after a 90-day trial period. Clarifying the AAF-AGF air defense dispute somewhat, he specifically charged the AAF with providing for the air defense of the united states and with the training and operational control of those antiaircraft artillery units assigned to the AAF. But this neither meant nor even assured assignment of such AGF units to the AAF. [43]

In June 1946, the AGF proposed a concept of "local ground defenses" and "air defense beyond the range of ground weapons", with the AGF being responsible for the former and the AAF for the latter. In effect, the AGF reasserted that air defense should be defined as "defense by air" and that division of control should be maintained. The AAF replied that air defense was a single mission which should not be divided., and that a single commander should control all units and weapons used for that purpose. The AGF then agreed on the need for unity of command but reiterated that air defense was only a part of overall defense of a nation. Since there was little likelihood of agreement at this time, the AGF suggested postponing further discussion until the General Staff ruled on the matter when it reviewed the results of the War Department 90-day reorganization trial period. [44]

Gen. Jacob L. Devers
Source: U.S. Army

The General Staff carefully studied the conflicting claims, could find no acceptable solution, and recommended retention of the status quo. Secretary Patterson and General Eisenhower approved this position on 24 September 1946, when they issued the final organization revision. The AAF retained the air defense mission and the training and operational control of AGF antiaircraft artillery units assigned to the AAF for defense of base installations, but not those still under AGF jurisdiction. [45]

Faced with the split mission in air defense and with AAF management of Army guided missile development (assigned to the AAF on 7 October 1946), General Spaatz and the AGF commander, Gen. Jacob L. Devers, tried on 9 October to reach a common understanding on their responsibilities. Later that day, Spaatz confirmed in writing to Devers his "policies and opinions" as earlier discussed. Spaatz classified guided missiles and conventional antiaircraft artillery as two distinct weapons. He conceded that artillery development and manning of units were AGF functions under current policies. Spaatz promised to develop guided missiles needed to meet legitimate AGF requirements and agreed that AAF development of a surface-to-air missile would in no way prejudice AGF's right to operate it. Only higher officials could decide on the proper operating agency after they evaluated a missile's performance and its ability to accomplish a particular function. [46]

Devers quickly dissented, especially on the distinction between guided missiles and antiaircraft artillery. Devers contended that this "doesn't seem to mean much as I don't believe you know, anymore than I do, what conventional antiaircraft artillery (as distinguished from guided missiles), could possibly mean." Citing recent AAF proposals to procure surface-to-air missiles to defend a major vital urban area, Devers then accused the AAF of already overstepping the limits of its air defense responsibility and concluded, "I am sure you must agree that this mission (local air defense) belongs to the Army Ground Forces". [47]

In his reply, Spaatz listed pertinent JCS definitions to support his statement that clear distinctions existed between the two types of weapons. However, apparently recognizing that there was little prospect for agreement, Spaatz simply reiterated his stand that the General Staff would have to make the operational assignment for each guided missile after it had been developed and evaluated against specific mission requirements. [48]

The conflict over operational responsibility for guided missiles did not reappear until after unification. In working out the initial Army-USAF transfer agreement during the summer of 1947 before the actual separation of the AAF from the Army took place, officials incorporated a loosely worded paragraph on missile operations which glossed over the controversial views of the AAF and AGF. They appeared interested in effecting a gigantic task peaceably and speedily and in letting the future take care of itself.

The AAF-Navy Missile Rivalry

Almost as intense as its postwar struggles within the Army for dominance in the missile field was the AAF's competition with the Navy. Many of the reasons for this rivalry lay outside the missile area but they influenced greatly the actions taken there by the two services. To the AAF, the Navy's air arm was a major irritant, contradicting its doctrine of the indivisibility of airpower. And the AAF also feared that the Navy posed a major threat to its air defense and strategic bombardment missions. For its part, the Navy was alarmed at the AAF's popularity and prestige, its singular ability to deliver the atom bomb, airpower's menace to the future of seapower, and possible loss of Navy air units in the event of military unification.

This high degree of mutual distrust would normally have brought AAF-Navy missile controversies into the open, but a number of mitigating factors worked against public airings. Guided missiles were still an insignificant part of the current difficulties facing each service. Moreover, the AAF could deal with the Navy only at arm's length, since the latter possessed organizational stature a niche above its own. Finally, the AAF used caution in its guided missile dealings with the Navy to forestall harmful effects on pending unification legislation.

On 23 April 1945, BAT radar guided glide bombs were dropped on Japanese shipping off Balikiapan, Borneo. Several Japanese ships were sunk or damaged. The BATs were launched from Navy PB4Y aircraft.

Photo courtesy of Smithsonian.

Even before the close of World War II, the Navy had embarked on a large and well-rounded missile development program. After the war, the Navy expanded the program's scope and aggressively pushed development. As early as August-September 1945, some Air Staff members voiced fear that the Navy intended to grab the most important peacetime mission--air defense of the United States--by conducting "the most active anti-aircraft guided missile program." They contended that the Navy would naturally fall heir to the mission if it were the first to produce and operate this type of missile. [49]

These initial warnings went largely unheeded. But in November 1945, General Arnold learned that the Navy three months earlier had asked the President for $50 million to build and operate a test range at Point Mugu, California. To Arnold, this action indicated "the start of Navy domination of the guided missile development. $50,000,000 is far to too much for a testing range to be used for one service. This to me is a definite danger signal." [50] When the AAF later opposed the request, Navy-AAF irritation increased.

Another aspect of rivalry concerned development responsibilities. On 13 February 1946, when Eisenhower directed WDGS and the three Army forces to re-examine the McNarney Directive, he asked Adm. Chester W. Nimitz, Chief of Naval Operations, to cooperate in making an equitable division of development responsibility between the Army and Navy. Eisenhower explained that he thought this was necessary to counter widespread claims of duplication of effort and wasteful spending. Nimitz readily agreed. [51]

On 4 March 1946, when Spaatz presented his proposed revisions to the McNarney Directive, he also commented on the Army-Navy question. He believed that in the interest of the national economy, the Navy should limit its activity to adapting Army-developed missiles for use on ships and naval aircraft. Readily acknowledging that the Navy would not accept this solution -- and probably quite properly -- Spaatz suggested expanded and closer liaison and cooperation as the only alternative. [52]

On 18 March, the Navy proposed that inter-service discussions on responsibility be deferred until a JCS committee completed its review of the Army and Navy missile programs. The Navy also believed that at such time as negotiations began, they should be controlled by two basic principles: primary development responsibility for a missile should rest with the service using it and centralization of development under a single agency would be inimical to efficiency, endanger adequate coverage, and hamper training and operational planning and use. [53]

The JCS committee completed its reviews of the Army and Navy missile programs as well as the development responsibility problem by late in April and recommended no changes to current assignments. Taking advantage of these findings, Nimitz then informed Eisenhower that a division of responsibility between the Army and Navy was premature and would impede rather than speed development of guided missiles. He conceded, however, that it was impossible for a service to finance development of all its requirements and urged that some agency with strong coordinating authority be used to insure a complete and non-duplicating program. As this was not done, the issue of responsibility remained unresolved, to the disappointment of the AAF.

General Dwight D Eisenhower
Source: U.S. Army

Yet another important area of AAF-Navy friction involved AAF attempts to establish and dominate a consolidated Army-Navy guided missile program, whereby one or the other service developed a missile to meet requirements of both. However, unable to gain control within the Army until October 1945 and apprehensive over pending unification legislation, the AAF frequently backed off, compromised, or decided to await a more favorable time to push its objective. As a result, the Navy became increasingly uneasy over the real intent of the AAF campaign for a consolidated program. To obtain a consolidated program, the AAF used the Aeronautical Board as a means. This joint AAF-Bureau of Aeronautics (BuAer) agency had been established in 1939 to secure cooperative and coordinated development in military aviation. Late in December 1945, the board created the Subcommittee for Pilot-less Aircraft and Guided Missiles (This was redesignated in December 1946 as the Guided Missile Subcommittee) under its Research and Development committee. When the subcommittee first met on 22 January 1946, AAF members looked askance at the Navy's broad program but reluctantly agreed that no unwarranted inter-service duplication existed. At the second meeting, in April, the subcommittee decided that discussion on allocation of development responsibilities should await the outcome of a JCS policy and program review then under way. [55]

Meanwhile, AAF headquarters had asked the Air Materiel Command (AMC) to review in detail the Army and Navy missile projects and cite all instances of duplication. After receiving the information, AAF representatives discussed the AMC findings with their Navy counterparts on 9 May. The conferees again agreed that at this early date the technical approaches under study warranted the apparent duplication. [56]

In reporting these results to AMC, an Air Staff member emphasized the AAF's continued discontent with the Navy's "very aggressive program." Not only did it place the Navy in an unduly strong position during unification negotiations but it interfered with the conduct of the AAF program by saturating contractors engaged in missile development. Others felt "that the Navy is doing all within its power to gain pre-eminence in the G[uided] M[issile] field, as they [sic] see in it a means for the Navy to continue to be a major operational service in the next war . " Despite these fears, the AAF continued to proceed cautiously until its management of the Army missile program and unification had been assured. [57]

Once assured of authority over Army missile development, the AAF renewed its efforts to effect a consolidated Army-Navy program. In September 1946, the Aeronautical Board's guided missile subcommittee again reviewed the two service programs and decided that some duplication existed, primarily in the study project area (very few projects had yet advanced to development status). The two services agreed that the board should select at an appropriate time the agency to continue each project into the "hardware" phase. A month later, the subcommittee decided on the first two steps of this procedure -- to obtain agreement on a list of types of missiles (surface-to-surface, sea-to-air, etc.) and on a mutually acceptable statement of military characteristics for each missile. [58]

The gains from this encouraging decision were soon lost because of revived Navy distrust and fear over the AAF's real objectives. At his 8 October press conference announcing assignment of the Army missile development program to the AAF, Symington took a jab at the Navy by stating that this would reduce duplication within the Army but only establishment of a single defense department could eliminate all missile duplication. About the same time, the Navy learned that the AAF wanted to reopen the question of development allocations with the recently activated Joint Research and Development Board's (JRDB) Committee on Guided Missiles. [59]

The extent of these fears and suspicions was best summarized during a presentation to his departmental superiors by Rear Adm. Dan V. Gallery, the Navy's top guided missile officer. "While on the subject of cognizance, I must not omit to mention our friends in the AAF. They have publicly announced that they should have exclusive cognizance of all guided missiles for all services. That is their party line and they have many and devious ways of advancing it. They may appear before Congress, the Bureau of the Budget, the Aero Board or the JRDB and argue about economy and elimination of wasteful duplication--but when you boil it all down, the main thing they are after is simply control of the whole national program. The AAF reminds me a lot of the Russians. They both have war records for which I have the utmost admiration but both figure they have to throw their weight around a lot or else the older and more firmly established Governments and services won't recognize them. Any proposal that they make must be examined very carefully in the light of the avowed intention of running the whole show. In the final analysis, they can't run the whole show,

Admiral Dan V Gallery
Source: U.S. Navy

because they are not qualified by experience or background to do it. You may think I'm a young Admiral -- but you ought to see some of their generals."

Gallery also asserted that the Navy would push development as much as possible, since guided missiles would make all conventional weapons obsolete, revolutionize warfare to a greater extent than any previous new weapon, and possibly "even perform the miracle of rescuing the battleship from the museum ." [60]

It was not surprising therefore that in the prevailing uneasy atmosphere, darkened further by the unification discussions, AAF efforts to obtain some kind of consolidated Army-Navy program bore little fruit. The Navy continuously "dragged its feet" readily admitting that it was deliberately using delaying tactics. In March 1947, six long months after the Aeronautical Board had decided to institute inter-service military characteristics statements and development, the two services finally agreed on the simple task of listing the types of missiles. It took another three months for the Navy, AGF, and AAF to approve a standard form upon which to state military characteristics. The AAF then pressed for the final step, preparation of inter-service military characteristics for each missile, but the Navy asserted that it was "impractical to proceed further at this time." And so matters stood until the demise of the Aeronautical Board early in 1948. [61]

A few joint statements of military characteristics were finally prepared, primarily because of the fund cuts of late 1946 and early 1947, On 2 January 1947, Army and Navy representatives agreed that these cuts dictated the shift of development responsibility for several similar projects to one agency. The AAF volunteered the first candidate for transfer: its hydrogen bomb guided missile. After the Navy promised to prepare military characteristics suitable to both services, the AAF shifted its project. In April 1947, the Navy suggested that some of its requirements be included in a rocket missile being developed by the Ordnance Department, and General Spaatz, in his role as manager of the Army development program, readily assented. [62]

Citing the two consolidated projects as steps in the right direction, Spaatz gently chided the Navy for its past delaying tactics: "It is satisfying to be able to consolidate Army and Navy efforts in this way and I feel more combined efforts can be initiated when the two services arrive at mutually acceptable characteristics for individual types of missiles." Although the Navy replied that the general principle established in the mergers contributed to effective coordination and economy of effort, it said nothing about mutually acceptable military characteristics. As noted above, the Navy two months later said that it wanted no part in across-the-board joint characteristics statements that would lead to a consolidated program. [63]

III THE NATIONAL GUIDED MISSILE PROGRAM

The guided missile controversy spread beyond intra-service and inter-service circles, primarily because of the fiction that a national guided missile program existed. The services normally enjoyed wide latitude in stating requirements for developing and producing weapons essential to their operations. The concept of formulating and conducting a single program was applied only to guided missiles. While atomic bomb development was also a single program, the services neither stated requirements for, developed, or produced the bomb and as a result of national policy, most of this work was placed under civilian authority in Jan 1947. Guided missiles received special treatment because of their impact on current concepts of warfare and on service missions and roles, their immense demands upon so many technologies, and their tremendous cost. But in no other area of weapons did one service possess so many means to question, hamper, delay, and even veto the efforts of another service. These powers stemmed in large part from departmental agencies established outside the military services to promote a national program but staffed largely with partisan military representatives under civilian chairmen. The results were not good.

Genesis of the National Program

The idea of a single guided missile program originated in June 1942 when the Joint Committee on New Weapons and Equipment (JNWE), an agency recently established by JCS, directed an ad hoc group to examine the status of "controlled missiles" and recommend an "American program." In making its report late in 1942, the group advised against creating any special organization to conduct a single program. It encouraged instead a coordinated effort, with the Office of Scientific Research and Development (OSRD) assisting the individual services.

Both JCS and OSRD accepted the suggestion, and on 9 December 1942 the National Defense Research Council (NDRC), a unit of OSRD, created its Division 5 -- the Division of New Missiles -- to work with the military. [1]

This system continued in use until 16 January 1945, when JNWE, in the wake of the McNarney Directive and inter-service coordination discussions, established the Guided Missiles Committee (GMC). Under its charter, GMC could formulate broad programs and recommend procedures to insure proper coordination of research and development among the military missile agencies. More specifically, GMC was expected to evaluate current projects and priorities, recommend a single development program, and propose suitable responsibility assignments. Two representatives from OSRD, one from the NACA and three each from the Army and Navy would comprise the membership. [2] In one form or another, GMC continued in existence until mid-1958, although its place in the defense establishment and its functions, powers, and influence fluctuated greatly.

31

General William A Borden
Source: U.S. Army

As if indicative of difficult days ahead, selection of Army representatives became quite troublesome. On 17 January 1945, General Borden, head of the New Developments Division, asked each of the three Army forces to choose a senior officer for membership on the committee. After learning that the three Navy appointees were staff rather than bureau members, he decided that the Army representatives should come from the General Staff. Explaining this reversal, Borden stated that GMC would consider broad policy matters only, making selections from WDGS more appropriate. The three Army forces objected, the AAF claiming that "the recommended representatives would be inadequate, restrictive and incompetent as regards the Army Air Force's interests." Nevertheless, Borden's selection of representatives from his division, G-3, and G-4 won General Marshall's approval. [3]

On 15 February 1945, WDGS asked the AAF to furnish an officer for the GMC secretariat. The AAF took this opportunity to question again the method of selecting the committee members and demand representation. General Borden, in conference, again explained the purpose of GMC and promised that it would not examine in detail missile operations, priorities, or responsibilities. Still concerned with the committee's scope of activity, General Giles asked Borden to confirm this in writing. At this time, learning that his interpretation was not entirely accurate, Borden shifted his position and recommended that GMC add representatives from the three Army forces. [4]

Policies For a National Program

Enlarged to 16 members and 14 alternates, the GMC began a survey of the various missile programs. Initially, it concentrated on missiles that might be used against the Japanese, and on 10 August, submitted its findings to JCS. GMC then turned to the matter of a postwar program. The committee first studied existing policies and plans and, by November, had prepared a draft policy to provide guidance in formulating a national missile program. [5]

GMC proposed that the services terminate virtually all of their wartime projects since they had been based on expedience, were of questionable worth in fulfilling requirements, and progress on nuclear warheads and propulsion would largely shape future missile development. GMC also proposed grouping guided missiles according to function:

- precision area attacks,

- precision pinpoint-target attacks

- destroying airborne targets

- defending coastal installations and ships from hostile naval and amphibious attacks

To obtain these sophisticated missiles, GMC strongly urged emphasis on fundamental research during the next few years and warned against a too-hasty shift to preparation of military characteristics statements and construction of operational prototypes. The reservoir of technical knowledge was low, the number of scientists and engineers limited, and the expense great. since another war did not appear imminent, a carefully phased program of research and then development would hardly endanger the nation's security. The services would have to balance this concept, however, against the ever-present need to modernize equipment and weapons. GMC said little on the important issue of allocating development responsibilities. It described current "rules of cognizance" between BuAer and Bureau of ordnance (BuOrd) and between the AAF and the Ordnance Department as "far from logical". But the committee did not elaborate on this point, suggesting only that the services make adjustments as new knowledge accumulated. [6]

JNWE approved the GMC report and its attached policy draft and on 5 February 1946 sent them to JCS. The AAF found little fault with the proposed policy but believed its consideration by JCS to be most inopportune. The General staff had just begun studying possible changes to the McNarney Directive, and Eisenhower had asked Navy cooperation in delineating departmental responsibilities.

Hopeful that these studies would lead to AAF management of Army, and perhaps all, missile development, General Spaatz on 5 March asked JCS to return the GMC report and policy draft until results of the departmental studies became available. The Navy opposed Spaatz's proposal, claiming that an interdepartmental policy was needed immediately to still charges of unwarranted duplication in the missile field. When the studies in progress were completed, GMC could recommend desirable changes to the policy. [7]

Concerned that a policy statement might unduly influence the findings of the studies, Air Staff planners asked Spaatz to continue his opposition. They suggested that he use the absence of responsibility assignments--essential in any statement of policy--to forestall JCS action. Should this fail, Spaatz could then ask that JCS first settle the missions and roles of the land, sea, and air forces. This was a question of utmost significance under study in JCS and it was of direct import to the missile program.

Despite these staff views, Spaatz joined the other members of JCS on 22 March 1946 in approving the GMC report and in asking Secretary of War Patterson and Secretary of Navy James V. Forrestal to issue the proposed policy for a national missile program. [8]

The two secretaries accepted the JCS recommendations and on 1 April officially issued the policy statement. It listed the four classes of missiles to be built and emphasized the need for fundamental research. Development would take place only after sound knowledge had been obtained. Patterson and Forrestal permitted some duplication of effort if the bureaus, corps, and departments closely coordinated this work and shifted responsibility as necessary. Finally, they called for comprehensive joint planning in procurement, testing, and training, in devising countermeasures and operational techniques, and in gathering intelligence data. [9]

The National Program and Development Responsibilities

The Patterson-Forrestal statement of 1April outlined a broad policy for conducting a national guided missile program but it did not create such a program. Nor did it resolve conflicts over development responsibility. Within a few weeks, however, Bradley Dewey, a leading industrialist serving as chairman of GMC, recommended that the responsibility problem be left unchanged. He concluded that service claims for missile development responsibility fell into four groupings,-operational, technical, administrative, and legal. All were valid but to give equal weight to each would only confuse the issue. He saw three possible solutions:

- assign all responsibility to one agency;

- use a specific set of rules to divide the missile field and avoid duplication;

- allow duplication but maintain a finely integrated program through an effective coordinating organization.

Dewey opposed the first possibility because it was difficult to select a single agency and such a step might prematurely limit the number of alternate technical approaches. He also ruled out the second, pointing to at least nine previous unsuccessful attempts to establish criteria for delineating responsibility, such as aerodynamic versus ballistic, short-range versus long-range, air-launched versus surface-launched, and strategic versus tactical. Many of these, he asserted, had been proposed solely to obtain control of the entire missile program. Dewey therefore recommended the third possible solution, explaining that "progress in the guided missiles field will be best promoted by having all the cognizant agencies now concerned continue their activities. The price of this solution will be the establishment of a coordinating agency stronger than any which has heretofore existed and the enunciation by the Joint Chiefs of Staff of certain definite military policies for the guidance of this group".

Dewey felt that healthy competition was desirable during the missile gestation period because each service could not maintain steady and rapid progress in all technical areas, and advances by one agency might overcome the lag of another. Thus Dewey recommended no change in program responsibilities but establishment of a powerful joint Army-Navy coordinating board, as earlier proposed by GMC in November 1945. He foresaw that "in the course of time and almost certainly within a few years changes of policy would be found desirable. These would depend upon the development of new knowledge--knowledge determined by technical research as well as the developments of military strategy and priorities incident thereto." The committee members accepted Dewey's views and the responsibilities question was temporarily set aside. [10]

Shortly after the policy and development responsibility statements were issued, GMC technical panels (subcommittees of military and civilian experts) reviewed the technical portions of each missile project under way. They found that both services had properly oriented their individual projects from a technical standpoint, as distinct from military requirements. Both were concentrating on fundamentals, although interspersed among research study projects were several with operational missiles as their immediate objective. The panels were unable to pass on the desirability of these "short-term" developments in terms of military necessity but warned that they might cause undue competition for funds, personnel, and facilities.

This division between research and "hardware" led to the panel's major conclusion: "Bluntly speaking, there seems to be no overall national plan for guided missiles." A missile program that assumed a war to be imminent should be radically different from one that anticipated a long period of peace. The services had based the current program on neither assumption nor even on a realistic combination of the two. They recommended that GMC, "in the absence of an overall national plan for guided missile development" strongly encourage the services to concentrate on basic research. [11]

Establishment of JRDB's Committee on Guided Missiles

JCS did not act on the recommendations of either Dewey or the technical panels, perhaps because they were overtaken by events, particularly a reorganization. The JNWE, the only joint wartime agency that exercised any real control over Army and Navy development programs, had often found its effectiveness limited by the need to obtain unanimous agreement among its members. Dr. Bush, JNWE's chairman, realized that the committee could not succeed in peacetime, when the pressures that induced unanimity would disappear. On 24 November 1945, Bush suggested that the President reconstitute the committee and empower it to oversee development work, allocate responsibility, and assign priorities. The alternative was to dissolve JNWE. Meanwhile, the services had recommended establishment of a special board under JCS jurisdiction. The Administration accepted neither proposal but established a new organization, the JRDB, directly responsible to the Secretary of War and Secretary of Navy. [12]

JRDB received its charter on 6 June 1946 and met formally for the first time on 3 July, with Dr. Bush as chairman and two members from each of the two services. At this time, Secretary of War Patterson emphasized that JRDB, acting for the two secretaries, would coordinate all research and development

Dr Vannevar Bush
Source: U.S. War Department

of joint interest to insure unified, integrated, and complete programming. The board could allocate to a single service responsibility "for specific programs of joint interest" but it had no authority to administer development activities or prevent gaps in programs, initiate or terminate projects, or establish priorities or magnitude of effort. While it enjoyed broader powers than its predecessor, JRDB nevertheless encountered difficulty in operating because it could deal only with developments of joint interest. On 15 August 1946, JRDB, in line with its plan to establish numerous subgroups, created the Committee on Guided Missiles, consisting of three civilian members from the scientific and industrial world and two representatives from each service. Two weeks later, JGS dissolved the Joint Committee on New Weapons and Equipment and its Guided Missile Committee. [13]

The AAF had little quarrel with the purposes of JRDB and its committees, including the Committee on Guided Missiles. Some Air staff officials thought that only through such groups could the AAF present its case, expect judicious decisions, and eventually gain control over most, if not all, of the guided missile programs. These hopes were ill-founded.

The AAF initially encountered difficulty in the selection of members for the numerous JRDB committees. Although it was virtually autonomous, especially in research and development, and its commander was a member of JGS, the AAF was considered as only a part of the Army for purposes of representation, even on those committees dealing almost exclusively with aeronautical equipment and weapons. The AAF contended that this was obviously unfair and unsuccessfully proposed that it have equal representation with the Army and Navy on certain committees. After taking over management of the Army missile development program in October 1946, the AAF again considered asking for increased representation on GMC, where only one of the seven members came from the AAF. After some indecision, Air Staff officials concluded that the matter required extremely "delicate handling" and decided not to seek a change "for the present time." Unification eventually supplied the answer to the equal representation problem. [14]

National Program Review by GMC

One of the more important tasks of the new GMC was the assignment of responsibility for projects of joint interest. An ad hoc group within GMC quickly settled the problem in February 1947, concluding that competition and duplication between services was healthy but should not be tolerated within a service. Consequently, a detailed division of responsibility was unnecessary. This basically reaffirmed the position taken by Mr. Dewey and the former GMC. The GMC planning consultants (replacements for the former GMC technical panels) enthusiastically endorsed these views when they completed their technical review of the national program on 1 May 1947. [15]

The planning consultants also agreed with recent project cancellations forced on the services because of funding cutbacks. The remaining projects constituted "a reasonably well balanced program" and technical progress had been good despite the many uncertainties of the postwar adjustments. The technical approaches of the Ordnance Department and BuOrd were noteworthy, both agencies having used a broad task base with wide latitude in objectives to provide a solid foundation for a stable long-term development program. The planners criticized BuAer and the AAF for pushing designs based on current data, which led to premature emphasis on statements of specific military characteristics. Both had recognized this fault and were correcting it.

Looking ahead, the consultants found that the major immediate problem concerned the AAF program. Of its 16 projects, only one was older than a year and the others were still in the study stage. Missile contractors expected to complete the studies by June 1947 but it was obvious that the AAF could not continue all of the projects into the hardware phase because of fund limitations. The technical balance of the national program would depend on the projects the AAF decided to continue. [16]

GMC approved the report and its recommendations even though an unbalanced national program might result when the AAF made its expected cutbacks. At the same time, paradoxically the committee ratified inter-service competition and duplication and declined to assign development responsibilities. Thus, when the AAF canceled additional projects there was the distinct possibility of a national program containing considerable competition and even duplication in some areas and major gaps in others. Lacking sufficient funds, the services would be unable to rectify the imbalance.

The National Program: Fact or Fiction?

When Mr. Dewey in April 1946 proposed a laissez-faire policy for missile development responsibility, he had presumed that JCS would furnish specific military guidance and create a strong coordinating agency. JCS did neither, for the subject of guided missiles apparently was not a topic on its agendas between March 1946 and mid-1949. The second GMC, despite its broad inherent powers, reaffirmed Dewey's policy. GMC and its supporting secretariat and panels, composed of military representatives and civilians with partisan service tendencies and vested interests, found objectivity extremely elusive and quite naturally avoided controversy where possible and sought compromises to problems that were unavoidable. Hence, during its existence from August 1946 to September 1947, GMC assiduously resisted all attempts to divide guided missiles among the contending service agencies and concentrated instead on reviewing and questioning the technical approaches being used for individual missile projects.

Since JCS was apparently disinterested and GMC weak, it was inevitable that each service would range broadly into all areas of guided missiles without fear of accountability. Only the lack of money imposed any restraint on duplication of effort. The national missile program was more myth than fact. It actually consisted of four programs, individually formulated and carried out by the Army's AAF and Ordnance Department, and the Navy's Bureau of Aeronautics and Bureau of Ordnance. Military unification, beginning in 1947, would not remedy the problem.

IV. AAF. POSTWAR GUIDED MISSILE PROGRAM

Following the German successes with their V-1 and V-2 missiles, the AAF intensified its interest in guided missiles and shifted part of its development effort from glide and vertical bombs to the more sophisticated self-propelled missiles. These initial changes in emphasis and technical approach provided the foundation for the AAF postwar guided missile development program. As a first step, AAF officials completed in mid-July 1944 a broad statement of military characteristics for four different groups of power-driven guided missiles:

- surface-to-surface
- surface-to-air
- air-to-surface
- air-to-air.

On 31 August 1944, the Materiel Command and Air Service Command had been combined as the Air Technical Service Command (ATSC). After considering revisions proposed by the Materiel Command, the Air Staff late in September directed the Air Technical Service Command missile program to proceed with the reoriented contained most of the old projects and emphasized missiles that might become operational before the war ended. ATSC could only carry out a small part of the planned work on the new projects before the Air Staff revised the program to give it a postwar outlook. [1]

Planning the AAF Postwar Program

With the increased attention to missiles late in 1944, General Arnold made a major readjustment to the unsatisfactory Air Staff organizational structure for these weapons. Responsibility for the few un-powered versions still in development remained with the Air Communications Office but responsibility for the remainder returned to normal staff channels. The several assistant chiefs of Air Staff would handle guided missiles as they did manned aircraft. [2]

The Assistant Chief of Air Staff for Operations, Commitments and Requirements (AC/AS, O, C&R) now undertook a complete review of the missile program. It concluded late in February 1945 that development suffered primarily from lack of suitable statements of requirements and of military characteristics. The "urgent" tag had been applied to virtually all missile projects, confusing ATSC on where to devote its major effort. There was obvious need for an orderly program of research through development to flight testing. AC/AS, O, C&R set out to remedy these shortcomings with a firm set of requirements for postwar missiles based on expected attainability within a given time period rather than on urgent tactical and strategic military factors.

As General McKee, the deputy chief, explained, "We are attempting to devise military characteristics capable of accomplishment within the next few years in terms of the 'state of the art.' We do not wish the impossible. At the same time, we would like to be sure that we have in fact asked the ultimate of which research and development is capable in the near future." [3]

In preparing the new statements, AC/AS, O, C&R was not unmindful of the current struggle with AGF and ASF for missile supremacy within the Army so the statements had the added purpose of supporting AAF claims for virtually all types of missiles:

- those launched from aircraft

- those complementing fighter-bombers in the attack of targets behind the immediate battleground

- those employed as interceptors, provided flight sustenance did not depend on momentum;

- those used for long-range strategic bombardment, including momentum (ballistic) missiles

- all others depending on a sustaining force other than momentum. [4]

By the end of April 1945, AC/AS, O, C&R had distributed the first draft of the military characteristics statements throughout the AAF and War Department for comment. Reception was generally good, although some critics thought their issuance premature and should await the close of war and the results of further research. Advocates of the statements pointed to the "uncontrolled and uncoordinated development program," and gained enough support to continue. A 2 May conference between Air Staff and ATSC officials settled major outstanding technical questions. Late in June, the Air Staff began issuing piecemeal military characteristics statements for individual and "families" of missiles. Between 26 June and 23 August 1945, AAF headquarters sent nine statements to ATSC and promised more. [5]

Inauspicious Start on Postwar Development Program

Shortly after V-J Day, Major General E. M. Powers, AC/AS-4, the new designation for the former AC/AS, Materiel and Services, took stock of AAF missile development and announced overall, long-term goals. On 10 September 1945, he told ATSC that the nine military characteristics statements covered approximately one-half of the planned program and the remainder would be sent as they received Air Staff approval. Because some officials, both in the Pentagon and at Wright Field, believed the goals far beyond current technical capabilities, Powers asked ATSC to provide comparative performance figures for these planned missiles, based on available components and similar equipment to be developed during the next five years. [6]

Almost simultaneously, General Powers blamed ATSC for shortcomings in pursuing program objectives. On 18 September, he contrasted the AAF postwar program -- virtually nonexistent except for the few approved statements of military characteristics -- with the well-advanced Navy and Ordnance Department programs. He attributed this to ATSC's decision to "sit back" and first observe the policies and trends of the other agencies and to the apathy and lack of initiative being carried over from the war when many Air Staff and ATSC top officials classified guided missiles as "Buck Rogers gadgets." Powers reminded ATSC of past actions taken by AAF headquarters to outpace the Navy and Ordnance, pointing to the statements of military characteristics for advanced missiles issued in July 1944 and their revisions between March and August 1945. He then directed ATSC to submit by 10 November a plan of current and contemplated actions on organization, personnel assignments and tours, training, contracts, industrial relationships, liaison, budget, and facilities. [7]

The attention that ATSC supposedly accorded the complaint "which was intended to emphasize the necessity of 'top-side' careful planning . . .' fell considerably short of Air Staff expectations. Reports reaching Washington indicated that ATSC had "bucked" Powers' letter to descending echelons within the Wright Field development organization through two generals and two colonels to a major who was Acting Chief of the Pilot-less Aircraft Branch. In this organization of 17 men, 13, including the acting chief, were awaiting demobilization. Preparation of the data sought by Powers was to be a one-man effort of this major who apparently was low man on the "totem pole". It Headquarters missile officials thereupon recommended that Powers personally discuss the matter with Major General Hugh J. Knerr, ATSC commander, and his staff to impress upon them "that the guided missile program will be a very large factor in the future (or lack of future) of the Army Air Forces. [8]

Air staff officers continued to criticize ATSC, pointing early in November to the nonexistence of postwar missile contracts and the apparent lack of a coordinated plan to get the program under way. Observing that contracts would probably not be awarded before February 1946, some 10 months after the original drafting of military characteristics statements, the Air Staff again called on ATSC for "more energetic prosecution of the Guided Missile program.[9]

Although ATSC did not defend its actions or lack of actions, the reasons were quite obvious. Most important was the hasty military demobilization and civilian reduction-in-force which wrecked the operational capability of the AAF and had similar effects on ATSC. The command also faced the problem of starting or enlarging development in areas revolutionized during the war -- atomic energy, jet propulsion, electronic guidance, etc. Funding was another stickler, for no one seemed to know how much was available for missiles. Much of the wartime missile effort had been done by the marginal companies in the aeronautical industry or by firms no longer interested in military contracts. For the postwar program, ATSC looked to the leading aircraft concerns--companies which during the war were not interested but who now were eager to participate. Thus, ATSC faced the task of starting anew with firms with no missile experience. "This transition to a new type of program," said ATSC, "is being pursued and will continue to be pursued energetically."
[10]

Despite the Air Staff fears, the information that ATSC furnished Powers on 26 November 1945 was comprehensive and authoritative. It related personnel, funding, and facilities difficulties and listed the steps ATSC had taken in getting the program under way. Most significant was that, starting late in October, ATSC had invited between 16 and 31 companies to bid on the study and preliminary design of each projected missile. [11]

In the following months, Wright Field's Engineering Division evaluated company proposals and selected winners. During March and April 1946, ATSC let a series of study and preliminary design contracts for the required missiles, allowing a study period of 8 to 18 months, but with the majority set at 12 months. During March, ATSC also terminated all but three of the remaining wartime missile projects. [12]

After nearly two years the AAF postwar missile program had finally advanced from the planning to the research and development stage. At the end of April 1946, it contained 12 surface-to-surface, seven air-to-surface, three surface-to-air, and 6 air-to-air missile projects. Although the program appeared comprehensive, it did not cover all AAF requirements

ARMY AIR FORCE GUIDED MISSILE PROGRAM APRIL 1946

Project	Contractor	Performance	Features
Surface-to-Surface			
MX-770	North American	175-500 miles	Winged rocket became Navaho
MX-771A	Glenn L Martin	175-500 miles	Subsonic became Matador
MX-771B	Glenn L Martin	175-500 miles	Supersonic
MX-772A	Curtiss-Wright	500-1500 miles	Subsonic
MX-772B	Curtiss-Wright	500-1500 miles	Supersonic
MX-773A	Republic	500-1500 miles	Subsonic
MX-773B	Republic	500-1500 miles	Supersonic
MX-774A	Convair	1500-5000 miles	Subsonic
MX-774B	Convair	1500-5000 miles	Supersonic
MX-775A	Northrop	1500-5000 miles	Subsonic became Snark
MX-775B	Northrop	1500-5000 miles	Supersonic became Boojum
MX-767	AMC	Modification of B-29 to drone became Banshee	
Air-to Surface			
MX-601	Douglas		Vertical bomb controllable in range and azimuth – became Roc
MX-674	Bell		Vertical bomb controllable in range and azimuth – became Tarzon
MX-776	Bell	100 miles	Subsonic became Rascal
MX-777	McDonnell	100 miles	Supersonic
MX-778	Goodyear	100 miles	Subsonic
MX-779	Goodyear	100 miles	Supersonic
Mastiff		300 miles	Supersonic, nuclear warhead
Surface-to-air			
MX-606	Boeing	35 miles; 60,000 feet	Became Gapa and Condor

MX-794	Michigan Univ	550 miles; 500,000 feet	Became Wizard
MX-795	General Electric	550 miles; 500,000 feet	Became Thumper
Air-to-Air			
MX-570	Hughes	9 miles, 50,000 feet	Subsonic, became Tiamat
MX-798	Hughes	5 miles	Subsonic
MX-799	Ryan	Fighter-launched	Subsonic, became Firebird
MX-800	Kellogg	Fighter-launched	Supersonic
MX-801	Bendix	Fighter-launched	Supersonic
MX-802	General Electric	Bomber-launched	Supersonic, became Dragonfly

The North American Navaho Missile in its final configuration Source: NASA

The Martin Matador Missile Source: U.S. Air Force

Northrop Snark – The only missile known to have missed the continent it had been aimed at. Source: U.S. Air Force

There remained several sets of approved military characteristics on which ATSC had taken no action. For example, development of extremely long-range surface-to- surface missiles (with 3 range categories between 5,000 and 13,000 miles) obviously awaited advances in the state of the art and substantial "hardware" development on surface-to-surface missiles with ranges to 5,000 miles. Action on the short-range missile (to 175 miles) awaited the conclusion of AAF'-AGF negotiations over mutually acceptable military characteristics. These were finally issued on 6 Jan 1947 but subsequent disagreement between the AAF and the Ordnance Department over who should develop the missile ended with a War Department General Staff decision directing the AAF to terminate its project and keeping the Ordnance Department project in a "study" stage. Eventually, the latter received approval for development. In addition, lack of funds or of essential technical data forced the AAF to keep several other contemplated missiles in abeyance. [13]

Black Christmas of 1946

An Air Staff review of the missile development program in the fall of.1946 resulted in only minor changes. This was not unexpected, since contractors were still in the midst of their studies. However, in the winter of. 1946, the AAF, received the first of many blows to its hopes of conducting an orderly development program, blows that eventually led to the discontinuance of all but a minute part of the original postwar program. During Christmas week, known at Wright Field as "the black Christmas of 1946", the president ordered a drastic cutback in fiscal year 1947 research and development spending, effective immediately. After hasty study, the Air Staff deleted more than 55 percent of the guided missile budget, reducing it from $29 million to $13 million. Ensuing discussions between the Air Staff and the Air Materiel Command (AMC) initially led to a recommendation to eliminate all of the 28 missile projects, and on 31 December, AMC began issuing termination orders to the affected contractors. Studies, appeals, rejustifications and reorientations of objectives during the next several months lightened the blow slightly. By the end of March, when the cutback details had finally been settled, the AAF had eliminated l0 projects and retained 19: 7 surface-to-surface, 5 air-to-surface, 3 surface-to-air, and 4 air-to-air. [15] One new project (MX-904) was established to replace two canceled projects (MX-570 and MX-298).

ARMY AIR FORCE GUIDED MISSILE PROGRAM MARCH 1947

Project	Contractor	Performance	Features
Surface-to-Surface			
MX-770	North American	500 miles	Winged rocket became Navaho
MX-771A	Glenn L Martin	500 miles	Subsonic became Matador
MX-772B	Curtiss-Wright	150 miles	Supersonic
MX-773B	Republic	1500 miles	Supersonic ramjet or rocket
MX-774B	Convair	5000 miles	Supersonic
MX-775B	Northrop	5000 miles	Supersonic became Boojum
MX-767	AMC	Modification of B-29 to drone became Banshee	

The U.S. Air Force & Guided Missiles

Air-to Surface			
MX-674	Bell		Vertical bomb controllable in range and azimuth – became Tarzon
MX-776	Bell	100 miles	Subsonic became Rascal
MX-777	McDonnell	100 miles	Supersonic
MX-778	Goodyear	100 miles	Subsonic
Mastiff		300 miles	Supersonic, nuclear warhead
Surface-to-air			
MX-606	Boeing	35 miles; 60,000 feet	Became Gapa and Condor
MX-794	Michigan Univ	550 miles; 500,000 feet	Became Wizard. Anti-ballistic missile weapon.
MX-795	General Electric	550 miles; 500,000 feet	Became Thumper. Anti-ballistic missile weapon.
Air-to-Air			
MX-799	Ryan	Fighter-launched	Subsonic, became Firebird
MX-800	Kellogg	Fighter-launched	Supersonic
MX-802	General Electric	Bomber-launched	Supersonic, became Dragonfly
MX-904	Hughes	Bomber-launched	Subsonic, generalized study

The Banshee Project was aimed at establishing an ultra-long range capability for the B-29 by flying the aircraft under remote control on a one-way mission. Flight tests of some guidance equipment in manned B-29s were conducted, but otherwise almost no information on the project is readily available. Project Banshee had a relatively low priority rating and it is unlikely that any unmanned B-29 flights took place. One B-29 involved in Project Banshee crashed in 1948, killing nine of the thirteen crew on board and the program was abandoned shortly afterwards. The basic concept was briefly revived in Project MX-1457 Brass Ring that would have used a remote-controlled B-47B

Source: U.S. Air Force

Dim Prospects for Fiscal Year 1948

The Boeing Gapa
Source: U.S. Air Force

As the AAF adjusted to its reduced missile program, it faced two additional major missile problems: criticism of the advanced technical features called for in the military characteristics statements and discouraging fiscal year 1948 funding prospects. With respect to the statements, AAF development experts questioned whether their technological demands were feasible. AC/AS-3 (Operations) defended them forcefully, asserting that in the past the statements had not asked enough and all too frequently the product had been only partially capable of meeting operational needs. Therefore, in formulating the missile statements AC/AS-3 had aimed for the ideal--weapons in advance of anything on hand and yet operationally possible. Technical feasibility was outside its purview. The AAF should retain the military characteristics statements as written but development officials should not use them as contract specifications, as they had been doing. Instead, based upon their knowledge of the state of the art, they should proceed to the goal by progressive stages, one grand leap, or an intermediate course. The ultimate missile objective should remain inviolate and compromised only as a last resort. [16]

General LeMay, Deputy Chief of Air Staff for Research and Development, accepted this concept as necessary to insure the nation's military superiority. In conveying his views to AMC on 17 March 1947, LeMay acknowledged that advances by progressive steps might prove necessary but that this was a matter for AMC to determine. If it decided on the step-by-step procedure, AMC would inform the Air Staff and await formal approval for any revision or waiver. [17]

Meanwhile, the AAF became increasingly concerned over financial support for missiles. On 18 March 1947, AMC warned that the expected fiscal year 1948 budget was inadequate, since contractors were ready to start fabrication of missile components and test vehicles. and costs would increase sharply. Early in May, AMC completed an extended study confirming its prediction. Although considering the current missile program "desirable and technically sound, " AMC found that it was far too large for the expected budget. Since an increase seemed unlikely, the only alternative was to reduce further the number of projects. Assuming that the AAF would spend about $22 million for missile development during fiscal year 1948 and each of the following six years, AMC recommended eliminating "insurance" missiles (primarily subsonic versions of supersonic missiles, an exception being Martin's MX-771A Matador), concentrating most money on missiles with the greatest promise of early availability, using one contractor to obtain a series of

46

progressively advanced missiles, and relying on the Navy and ordnance for some of the required missiles. [18]

The Air Staff found little fault with the AMC-recommended program, and on l5 June 1947, General Spaatz approved it without change. The reoriented AAF guided missile program now included 15 projects, of which 4 were tentative and had to await suitable advances in the state of the art and their still-to-be-developed predecessors, two were slated for "prolonged study," and two were carryovers from World War II. This left the AAF with only seven major development projects. In the readjustment, seven projects had been canceled or downgraded. from missile to component development. [19]

ARMY AIR FORCE GUIDED MISSILE PROGRAM JULY 1947

Project	Contractor	Performance	Features
Surface-to-Surface			
MX-770	North American	500 miles	Supersonic winged rocket Navaho I
MX-771A	Glenn L Martin	500 miles	Subsonic turbojet became Matador
	North American	1,500 miles	Supersonic ramjet Navaho II
MX-775B	Northrop	5,000 miles	Supersonic turbojet became Boojum
	North American	5,000 miles	Supersonic nuclear ramjet Navaho II
MX-767	AMC	Modification of B-29 to drone became Banshee	
Air-to Surface			
MX-674	Bell		Vertical bomb controllable in range and azimuth – became Tarzon
MX-776	Bell	100 miles	Subsonic became Rascal
Mastiff		300 miles	Supersonic, nuclear warhead
Surface-to-air			
MX-606	Boeing	35 miles; 60,000 feet	Became Gapa and Condor
MX-794	Michigan Univ	550 miles; 500,000 feet	Prolonged study; became Wizard. Anti-ballistic missile weapon.
MX-795	General Electric	550 miles; 500,000 feet	Prolonged study; became Thumper. Anti-ballistic missile weapon.
Air-to-Air			
MX-799	Ryan	Fighter-launched	Subsonic, became Firebird
	Ryan	Fighter-launched	Supersonic, became Firebird
MX-802	General Electric	Bomber-launched	Supersonic, became Dragonfly

Establishment of Missile Priorities

The Tarzon Guided Bomb. A legacy program from WW2, Tarzon was used in the Korean War to destroy bridges.

Source: U.S. Air Force

Concurrent with the reductions, the AAF issued policy guidance on priorities, for it realized that peacetime budgets would not adequately cover even the limited development program. By using priorities, the Air Staff hoped to obtain at least those missiles most urgently needed to meet AAF operational requirements for the next 10 years. General Vandenberg, Deputy Commanding General, approved the guidance on 18 June 1947.

AAF planners gave top priority to bomber-launched air-to-surface and air-to-air missiles, on the assumption that supersonic bombers and long-range surface-to-surface missiles would not become operational during the next decade and that subsonic bombers would continue as the primary strategic delivery system. Since these aircraft had to be able to penetrate the air defenses that the enemy would have after 1952 and return successfully, they urgently required air-to-air missiles to fend off attacking fighters and missiles as well as air-to-surface missiles to destroy ground-based segments of the enemy air defenses and to permit stand-off bombing.

Second priority went to short-range (to 150 miles) surface-to-surface missiles because AGF urgently requested improved support weapons and the AAF expected to have operational versions available by 1952. The AAF did not have this type of missile under development, WDGS having forced its cancellation. However, the Ordnance Department was developing such a missile to meet AAF-AGF military characteristics and supposedly both forces would use it.

Air defense missiles (fighter-launched air-to-air and surface-to-air) and detection and warning systems had third priority on the premise that the Russians would have long-range bombers and missile-equipped submarines to deliver atomic weapons on the U.S. by 1952. Long-range strategic surface-to-surface missiles received fourth priority. This was a concession to the economic facts of life and the anticipated development period of at least 10 years. In the lowest priority were the wartime-originated interim air-to-surface "missiles" (vertical bombs).[20]

These priorities clearly indicated that the AAF viewed guided missiles as having only an auxiliary, not a primary, role in air operations during the coming decade. Planners expected to rely on the subsonic bomber and optimistically hoped that missiles might improve aircraft performance and help it survive. For air defense, the planners imposed the same task on missiles -- to augment or improve fighter aircraft capabilities, not replace them. Severe technological problems and austere budgets obviously caused their cautious guided missile approach. What part the natural trust in aircraft and the inherent distrust in still-to-be-proved unmanned missiles played in the priority determinations would be difficult to assess.

The Mastiff Fiasco

The Very Early Stages of a Nuclear Initiation.
Source: Manhattan Engineering District Project

One interesting phase in the AAF guided missile program began shortly after the atomic bombing of Hiroshima on 6 August 1945, when the AAF sought a speedy mating of atomic warheads and guided missiles. From the beginning, however, the AAF could not penetrate the wall of secrecy built by the Manhattan District and its successor, the Atomic Energy Commission (AEC) that had replaced the Manhattan District on 1January 1947. Vital information essential to AAF's optimistic plans stayed locked in Manhattan District vaults. Whether access to it would have led to the combination in the face of current technological uncertainties must remain a matter of conjecture.

Within a few hours after the Hiroshima bombing, Air Staff development officers were studying the feasibility of combining the atomic bomb with guided missiles. Top AAF officials, however, regarded this as premature, since access to atomic data awaited completion of policy discussions among American, British, and Canadian government leaders. One month later, a second attempt, this time by AC/AS-3, met a similar fate, although in this instance WDGS asked Manhattan District for the required information. When

General Powers, AC/AS-4, on 10 September furnished ATSC with the objectives of the AAF long-term missile development program, he pessimistically reported: "Specific application of atomic power uses to guided missiles development must be withheld until a governmental policy has been determined concerning the dissemination of information on atomic power." He added that in letting contracts, ATSC should omit all consideration of the use of atomic energy. [21]

The injunction was short-lived. On 18 October 1945, General Arnold inadvertently lifted the embargo while testifying before a Senate subcommittee on pending research legislation. In an "off-the-cuff" remark to a senator's query, Arnold alluded to the possibility of an immediate mating. By adding wings, a propulsion unit, and TV equipment, an atomic bomb would become a guided missile that could be air launched against targets up to 300 miles away. Assuming that Arnold believed the modification could be done with existing components, Air Staff officers readied within 24 hours a statement of military characteristics based almost entirely on his remarks and assigned the job a 1-B priority. General LeMay, in his role of a War Department military adviser to the Manhattan District, approved the requirement on 8 November. On 9 January 1946, AC/AS-4 finally sent it to ATSC for study and comment and asked for a reply by I February. [22]

General Leslie R Groves
Source: United States Army

Meanwhile, the stringent restrictions on the release of atomic information continued despite AAF efforts to lift them. This prompted Brig. Gen. Laurence C. Craigie, chief of ATSC's Engineering Division, to write to Maj. Gen. Leslie R. Groves, head of Manhattan District, on 6 December 1945. Observing that prominent public officials believed that other nations could develop nuclear-equipped missiles within five years, Craigie warned that the U.S. might lose its military superiority, unless the AAF immediately adapted atomic weapons to guided missiles, especially the surface-to-surface type. He explained that in their studies missile designers were making purely conjectural space allocations for a 2,000-pound. warhead and that they needed accurate information on space, weight, temperature, pressure, acceleration, fusing, and other bomb-housing requirements but no specific details about the bomb itself. This request was significant in several respects. The officer responsible for developing AAF's future weapons was relying at least in part on public statements for guidance in directing his program. He apparently possessed no accurate knowledge about the size, weight, or other features of the atomic bomb. Nor did he seem to know of the Air staff intent to develop an air-to_ surface missile with an 11,000 pound atomic warhead. [23]

Craigie's request prompted the Air staff to assure ATSC that some progress was being made in breaking down the information barrier and that security procedures were being established. In February 1946, the Air staff asked ATS. to prepare a comprehensive report on all projects involving the use of atomic energy to acquaint Manhattan District with AAF plans and promote a two-way flow of information. Meanwhile, AMC's Aircraft Laboratory completed the air-to-surface missile study on 1 March 1946 and predicted no major difficulty in developing the missile or modifying the launching airplane. Learning this promising news, the Air Staff on 29 March directed AMC to solicit work bids from industry. The project,

Major General
Laurence Craigie
Source: U.S. Army

designated Mastiff, was destined to have an ignominious existence and then disappear almost unnoticed. [24]

Establishing Project Mastiff was easy; getting it under way was not. Less than a week after the Air Staff had authorized the project, Craigie reported that AMC could not solicit proposals from the four potential contractors until Manhattan District supplied the information he had requested from Groves on 6 December 1945. AC/AS-4 appealed to LeMay for assistance, observing that planning for nuclear-equipped guided missiles had started in August 1945 but was then suspended pending a firm information policy. Eight months had now elapsed and the AAF was without adequate data or any assurance that the Manhattan District was acting on its requests. On 17 April 1946, LeMay again asked Manhattan District to supply the information and authorize its release to the four prospective Mastiff contractors. Meanwhile, after waiting more than a month without a reply, Craigie suspended Project Mastiff and notified his Pentagon superiors. [25]

LeMay's request of 17 April failed to effect the release of information, but Groves agreed to meet with AAF representatives on 22 May, At that time, he promised to supply the information if the AAF would establish a highly complex security system with exacting personnel investigations, tight control procedures, and physical separation of cleared personnel (AAF and contractor) from their coworkers. Details of this system, including creation at Wright Field of the Engineering Division Coordinating Office for Manhattan Project with Col. John R. Sutherland as chief, were worked out during the summer of 1946. [26]

On 4 September, Craigie optimistically renewed his request for warhead data but again without success. Manhattan District apparently was not completely satisfied with the security procedures. Discussions in October produced modifications that AMC reluctantly accepted after terming them impractical. on 4 November, it again requested the atomic data, but again there was no reply. Early in December, Craigie turned to the Air Staff for assistance, declaring that the security system was unworkable and that even greater difficulties could be expected when AEC, its Division of Military Applications (DMA) and the Military Liaison committee (MLC) replaced the Manhattan District on I January 1947. Craigie dishearteningly added that the guided missile program was "in bad shape", for want of atomic data. [27]

On 12 December 1946, Groves finally replied to AMC's requests of 4 September and 5 November. He assured AMC that "the Manhattan Project desired to provide the Air Forces with the information necessary to proceed with the development of controlled missiles employing atomic warheads" and proposed the visit of three previously cleared AMC officers to Sandia Base to prepare a plan of procedures and draw up a specification for warhead installation. [28]

AMC representatives went to New Mexico but came away with little data. Colonel Sutherland reported that AEC was primarily interested in using AMC's information requests as a test case in the establishment of policies and procedures for the release of data. AEC officials had suggested that AMC create a unit with the sole function of designing aircraft and guided missiles slated as atomic-weapon carriers. The AEC also insisted that the AAF must not break down the atomic bomb and place its components throughout a missile. The bomb, less its tail, had to be used intact.

Sutherland claimed that the first proposal wag unreasonable because it was too costly and difficult to assemble a large staff of qualified people to perform the specialized design work. The prohibition against "breaking up the bomb" would result in inefficient missile systems. Instead of the special design unit, Sutherland suggested that AMC send representatives to AEC and obtain whatever information the commission made available. These officers would then examine and make changes to contractor designs without divulging the information. Sutherland admitted that this procedure would be cumbersome and the explanation for design changes so sketchy as to be worthless to contractors. [29]

Sutherland's report led Craigie on 29 January 1947 to review Project Mastiff with AAF headquarters. The statement of military characteristics was now 15 months old, but AMC was still unable to take even the first step: "to request industry to submit proposals." It had no warhead information available, and the many attempts to obtain data "have so far been to no avail." Accordingly, Craigie questioned the validity of the Project Mastiff directive of. 29 March 1946. If AAF headquarters insisted on continuing the project, he needed to know when the pertinent atomic information would be available and if it could be passed to the contractors. [30]

AC/AS-4 drafted a reply conceding that security procedures were unduly restrictive, that AEC would probably not relax them for a year or more, and that perhaps from the standpoint of broad national policy relaxation was not desirable. On the other hand AEC's proposal to provide an installation specification would work if fully exploited and if AMC did certain duties normally performed by the contractor. Before the letter was dispatched, however, AC/AS-4 learned from MLC that work on the installation specification and the clearance procedures had been delayed. Therefore, on 25 February 1947, AC/AS-4 informed AMC that until the AAF received the specification, re-scheduled for 1 July 1947, the Mastiff directive was temporarily suspended. [31]

While the history of Project Mastiff was unfortunate, of more significance was the confusion in the atomic-weapon area which it so clearly revealed. Nor were these unsatisfactory conditions short-lived. Almost two years after the close of World War II, Lt. Gen. Nathan F. Twining, AMC's commander, complained bitterly about the restrictions imposed by security. He appealed to the Chief of Staff for assistance in removing security blocks and in shortening information channels between AMC through AAF headquarters and MLC to AEC. The alternative, Twining warned, was to accept a delay in the development of all aircraft and missiles designed to deliver atomic weapons. [34]

General Nathan F Twining.
Source: U.S. Air Force

Much of this pessimism also pervaded the Air Staff. In September 1947, a development staff officer observed that conditions were "gradually growing worse" and despite AAF efforts "we are today exactly where we stood on 6 August 1945, as far as atomic weapons are concerned." AEC was not developing an atomic warhead; neither was the AAF developing a missile specifically for delivery of atomic warheads. He attributed the impasse to four major reasons: AEC's overly restrictive interpretation of the Atomic Energy Act of 1946, AAF's (and MLC's) lack of initiative in pressing AEC to meet its military development functions, lack of workable security procedures, and AAF's reluctance to take aggressive action with AEC in other atomic areas in fear of jeopardizing its Nuclear Energy Propulsion for Aircraft (NEPA) project. [35]

The AAF kept Project Mastiff inactive through most of 1947. During October, however, as part of an overall guided missile program review, the newly independent Air Force dropped the "quick and dirty" approach suggested by General Arnold in his off-hand remark some two years earlier. New military characteristics replaced the old and the Aircraft Laboratory made another feasibility study. When the findings were in, the Air Force decided to keep

Project Mastiff at a very low rate of effort, awaiting further advances in the missile state of the art. In time, these advances overtook Mastiff itself. Beset with virtually impossible conditions from the first, because of AAF's inability to obtain any meaningful information from the Manhattan District and AEC, Mastiff never progressed beyond the most preliminary stage. Its funding depicted this most graphically. In fiscal year 1946, the AAF spent $4,918, the cost of the original Aircraft Laboratory feasibility study. It programmed $5 million for fiscal year 1947 but in October 1946 shifted $1 million to other work. During the "Black Christmas" cutback of December 1946, funding was reduced to $330, 000, and finally in February 1947, following the decision to suspend the project temporarily, the remaining funds were transferred elsewhere. Similar bit-by-bit reductions wiped out $1 million that the AAF had planned to use in fiscal year 1948. [33]

The impasse posed a serious hazard to the nation's security. Another Air Staff officer pointed out that the AAF expected to complete development of the Gapa air defense missile within two years (by 1949), and "if we can do this, so can our enemies." At that time, he added, "It will be impossible to get the atomic bomb to a specific target by conventional aircraft." Although obviously overstating the efficacy of the expected 1949 air defense system, the officer posed the serious problem of "a very fine bomb being produced which cannot be used," and he argued that the only immediate solution was development of a guided missile as an atomic-weapon carrier. [36]

After the AAF became an independent service in September 1947, it did not press AEC for information required for guided missile development. It failed to do so even after many of the guided missile military characteristics statements, revised during October-November 1947, called for atomic warheads, Not until 1949 was the "marriage" seriously considered again, and the Army, not the Air Force, provided the impetus.

V. THE FIRST 18 MONTHS OF UNIFICATION

On 26 July 1947, the President signed the National Security Act of 1947 providing for greater military unification through creation of the National Military Establishment (NME) under a Secretary of Defense. The act abolished the War Department, replacing it with the Department of the Army and the Department of the Air Force. On 18 September, the AAF became the United States Air Force, successfully concluding its long struggle for independence and a status of equality with the Army and Navy.

The National Security Act altered the functions and organizational placement of many existing defense agencies and established important new ones. In addition to the Office of the Secretary of Defense (OSD) and the three military departments and Services, there were now the National Security Council, the War Council, the Joint Chiefs of Staff, the Joint Staff, the Research and Development Board (RDB) and the Munitions Board, Each would influence inter-service relationships in the guided missile field and affect the USAF program. [1]

Redefining Service Missions and Roles

The most immediate task of the reorganized defense establishment was the transfer of funds, facilities, personnel, and functions from the Army to the Air Force. On 15 September 1947, a document entitled "Army-Air Force Agreements as to the Initial Implementation of the National Security Act of 1947" was issued. Shortly thereafter it was approved by James V. Forrestal, first Secretary of Defense. Several short paragraphs dealing with guided missiles represented an interim compromise of views between the two services. Of greatest importance to the future of the Air Force guided missile program, however, was the subject of missions and roles. The National Security Act prescribed only in broad terms the mission of each military service, omitting any reference to specific roles or functions. The President attempted to deal with this issue by defining the functions of the JCS and the services in his executive order of 26 July 1947. [2]

James V Forrestal
Source: U.S. Department of Defense

As subsequent events indicated, the order was too general to allay competition among the services. They were simultaneously under pressure to rebuild their strength to meet the exigencies of the cold war instigated by the Soviet Union and reduce military expenditures to meet the demands of an economy-minded

President, Congress, and public. A heated battle for scarce funds ensued, exacerbating the tendency of the services to enhance their positions within the defense establishment. Inevitably each interpreted the generalized missions and roles statements to its own benefit, seeking support from Congress and the public. The intense rivalry extended to the JCS and military departments who demonstrated an inability to divide the military appropriation "pie" amicably. In the words of Forrestal, "unification was failing to unify." [3]

The inadequacies of the Presidential executive order led Forrestal to meet with the JCS on the missions and roles issue at Key West, Florida from 11 to 14 March 1948 and reach some broad, basic decisions. Primary and collateral functions of the Army, Navy, and Air Force were described in greater detail and defined more precisely than in the earlier "functions" document. At the President's direction, Forrestal. on 21 April 1948 issued the result of the proceedings as a formal executive order. Known as the "Key West Agreement", this document was the principal guide on service responsibility for the ensuing decade. Forrestal subsequently approved a JCS memorandum for the record which asserted that the Key West Agreement was not a command or operational paper but "would serve mainly as guidance for planners." Nevertheless this functions paper, became the most important single document of the Defense Department. [4]

The Key West Agreement had little immediate effect on guided missile programs, which were still largely in the research and development stage. Beginning in mid_1949, however, operational questions arose and efforts to resolve them depended increasingly upon the interpretation of the agreement.

Missile Development Responsibility

The first post-unification guided missile problem concerned Army -- Air Force development responsibilities. The two services quickly agreed to adhere temporarily to the system adopted in October 1946. The Air Force would continue administering the programs of both services as if they were one, and the Army Director of Research and Development would replace the former WDGS Director of Research and Development as the umpire in inter-service disputes. Both services expected to keep these procedures until the reorganized Research and Development Board and its committee on Guided Missiles began functioning. [5]

After six months, the Army on 3 March termed this arrangement "embarrassing" particularly in its relationship with the reconstituted RDB and asked to terminate it. The Air Force readily agreed but thought the two services should retain most of the existing procedures for program cooperation, coordination, and liaison. A joint adjustment regulation issued on 22 June 1948 announced the administrative separation, effective 20 March. Suitable coordinating and liaison procedures were also agreed to at a meeting on 26 May.[6]

Meanwhile, the new RDB called for by the National Security Act of 1947 replaced the Joint Research and Development Board. Established on 30

September 1947, the new board enjoyed considerably broader powers than its predecessor which had been able to act only on matters of joint service interest. The RDB was not so limited and could consider all facets of research and development, joint or otherwise. [7]

The former Chairman of both JRDB and its predecessor, JNWE, Dr. Vannevar Bush, was retained to head RDB. Bush explained that RDB's most important duty was to create a single coordinated development program for all the services without duplication or research gaps. The board would work closely with JCS and keep it informed of development trends so that it could evaluate the military implications of advances in the state of the art. Bush considered the procedure a major innovation as it marked the first time that this country had adequate machinery for conducting research and development in the light of strategic requirements. [8]

Like JRDB and JNWE, RDB also established a new GMC. Reconstituted late in 1947, the committee consisted of three civilians, including the chairman, and two military representatives from each service. Under its charter approved on 3 February 1948, GMC could establish program goals, determine if there was duplication of work or research deficiencies, assess the adequacy of facilities and personnel, and insure coordination of the national program and service missile budgets. The charter did not specifically authorize GMC to allocate development responsibility among the competing services although such authority apparently existed as a by-product of other charter provisions. It was the first major question that arose. [9]

In its annual guided missile report on 9 June 1948, the Technical Evaluation Group (TEG), an advisory body which had replaced the Planning Consultants after unification, held that there could be sincere and effective cooperation among the service missile development agencies only if GMC clearly defined individual areas of responsibility. TEG proposed a delineation based on the mission of each service. The Navy and Air Force would develop air-launched missiles; the Army and Navy surface-to-air and short-range surface-to-surface missiles; and the Air Force (and the Navy as necessary) long-range surface-to-surface missiles. TEG saw no need to transfer projects already under way which did not fit this pattern but recommended that GMC approve a new missile project only if it were in accordance with this delineation. [10]

The two Air Force members of the GMC opposed TEG's proposal. Pointing to the exclusion of the Air Force from developing surface-to-air missiles, they emphasized that under both the Army-Air Force agreements of 1947 and. the Key West Agreement, the air defense of the United States was primarily the job of the Air Force. They had no comment, however, on the TEG proposal to assign short-range surface-to-surface missiles to the Army, perhaps because they made a distinction between pilot-less aircraft and guided missiles which, in the terminology of the Army-Air Force agreements of 1947, were two different weapons. [11]

At a meeting on 15 September 1948, GMC was unable to agree on either the TEG proposal or on any other basis for making missile development assignments. TEG had suggested a criterion based on military missions alone but some GMC members thought that such factors as potential users, technical competence, and available manpower and facilities also deserved consideration. An Air Force member, Brig. Gen. William L. Richardson, subsequently argued strongly that the mission of a service should dictate the assignment of both development and operational responsibilities with the latter the major determinant in assigning the former. [12]

GMC indicated its inability to agree in its December report to the RDB. GMC stated that it would make missile development assignments only as necessary by individual project based on the several factors listed by GMC members at the September meeting. RDB tacitly agreed on 16 December when it announced a policy on responsibility applicable to the entire field of military research and development. Assignments were necessary only for specific projects or programs of joint service interest. Criteria for such assignments were the service operational responsibilities defined by the JCS, single-service procurement agreements approved by the Munitions Board, and the capabilities of a service (in terms of personnel, facilities, and workload) to undertake a particular project, Thus, for the same reasons as its predecessor committees, the new GMC displayed an inability and a lack of eagerness to grapple with the problem of guided missile development responsibility. Subsequent events within the JCS and OSD virtually forced GMC to relinquish its authority in this area. [13]

Louis A Johnson
Source: U.S. Department
of Defense

The importance the three services attached to obtaining missile development responsibility was readily understandable. Assuming that "possession was nine points of the law," they saw the possibility of obtaining a function by first developing the weapon with which to accomplish it, the Key West Agreement notwithstanding. They also recognized that if GMC approved one project and not another, one service would have stronger claims to a particular mission and increased funds. But the rivalry was not without its price.

With military programs and appropriations subject to increasing scrutiny, the failure to settle the missile development issue inevitably led to duplication of work. This made the program suspect to top civilians in the Defense Department, especially after the appointment early in 1949 of Louis Johnson as the new Secretary of Defense.

Missile Operational Responsibility

As difficult but less pressing was the problem of missile operational responsibility. The Army-Air Force agreement of 15 September 1947 that implemented the National Security Act had dealt in part with the command and operation of guided missiles. With respect to the surface-to-surface type, it gave the Air Force control over "pilot-less aircraft" and strategic missiles. The latter was defined as missiles employed against targets whose destruction would not directly affect Army tactical operations. The Army controlled tactical missiles, defined as those supporting land operations and used against targets whose destruction would directly affect Army tactical operations. With respect to surface-to-air types, the Air Force would control area air defense missiles and the Army security missiles (i.e., those protecting Army field forces from air attack). Both services therefore could utilize surface-to-surface and surface-to-air missiles, but for specific purposes. [14]

This agreement was unique in that it existed at all. Before unification, the War Department General Staff as well as the AAF and AGF had tried unsuccessfully on numerous occasions to delineate service missile operational responsibilities. The 1947 agreements were reached only by keeping the terms of reference broad, omitting several highly controversial topics, and making distinctions for which there were no precedents. They stated that the Army-Air Force missile operational responsibilities would continue to be those previously in effect although there had never been an official division of the responsibilities. Again, for surface-to-surface missiles, the two services distinguished between "guided missiles" and "pilot-less aircraft, " a practice not consistent with official terminology but which conveniently sidestepped the matter of using pilot-less aircraft for close support. [15]

Although the agreement reaffirmed antiaircraft artillery operational policies set forth in a Spaatz-Devers agreement of July 1947, it was silent on the divergent Army-Air Force views concerning the use of missiles for point air defense. (The Army claimed that such missiles were merely antiaircraft artillery weapons; the Air Force disagreed.) By alluding only to the role of the missile in area air defense and in protecting Army field forces from attack, the agreement carefully skirted the issue of area-vs-point defense. [16]

The 1947 agreement, whatever its inadequacies, served as policy guidance until mid-1949 because the Army and Air Force did not particularly concern themselves with the problem of missile operational responsibility until that time. Opportunities to change it were not energetically pursued. In June 1948, General Aurand of the Army suggested to General Norstad that the Army and Air Force revise the missile operational provisions of the agreement. The Air Staff then proposed that the War Council (composed of JCS and the departmental secretaries) adopt a policy statement which would deal with the problem in an oblique manner. The policy statement drafted by the Air Staff classified all guided missiles as common-end items, available to each service in accordance with their assigned missions and roles. It thus anticipated continuing budget cuts which would prevent a service from developing all the types of missiles it needed and was in consonance with the Key West Agreement which called for the fullest utilization and exploitation of a weapon, no matter the developing service. JCS would assign the missile to the services if they required it. The Air Staff sent the proposed statement to Secretary of the Air Force Symington who took no action on it, apparently because he believed that it merely spelled out for guided missiles certain broad policies already in existence. [17]

U.S Navy Loon Missile Fired From Submarine USS Carbonero.
Source: U.S. Navy

During mid-1948, some USAF officers also warned with little effect that the Navy's large missile development program threatened to infringe on Air Force operational functions. Following a group tour of guided missile installations, Lt. Col. Robert C. Richardson, the Air Force representative of the Joint Strategic Planning Group (JSPG) within JCS, reported that the Navy's missile development effort far surpassed the Air Force's. The Navy's objective, he said, was to gain "dominance in all types of missile warfare and subsequent absorption of the strategic offensive role." Pointing to sizable Navy expenditures for missiles, Richardson concluded that the "return from these investments will no doubt pay off in ultimate roles in the field in direct ratio to the capabilities of the various interested parties." [18]

Air Staff development officials agreed with this view but saw no remedy for the condition as long as the USAF guided missile effort had to compete with the higher priority 70-group aircraft program then under way. Characterizing past attempts to obtain more missile funds as "one of the most frustrating experiences," the Directorate of Research and Development warned that unless additional money was found "we must be satisfied with the secondary role in the guided missile picture for which we are presently headed." [19]

Top Air Staff officials recognized that the Navy's missile program went "far beyond the scope of its [Navy] mission and roles" but they were unwilling to challenge the program in the RDB or JCS, the logical places for such action. Instead, they furnished their evidence to an OSD management committee, chaired by General McNarney, for use during an impending budgetary review of defense requirements. McNarney subsequently returned the data without comment. [20]

GMC and the National Missile Program

As earlier indicated one of the main tasks of RDB's Committee on Guided Missiles was to establish and maintain a balanced national missile development program. The task was not easy, particularly as the missile projects advanced to the stage of constructing components and test vehicles. Demand for funds became greater, but inadequate appropriations and frequent budget cuts were still the vogue. There were also problems arising from the make-up of the GMC. The military members quite naturally desired program adjustments only in order to meet the requirements of their respective services. The civilian members, reluctant to exercise their full authority, were markedly "unwilling to oppose energetically unilateral actions taken by the military services." In time, GMC restricted its activities largely to studying and questioning the technical portions of individual projects. It tended to accept virtually any compromise, suitable or not, when it shaped the form and content of each service's missile program which, together, constituted the national Program. This lack of vigorous leadership appeared to be a carry-over from the practices of the first GMC as well as its own decision not to tamper with service missile responsibilities.

Several examples depict GMC's generally ineffectual influence. During March 1948, the Air Force considerably altered its missile development program, and GMC learned of it only indirectly. The matter "came to a rather violent head" during the meeting of 6 April, when the GMC chairman charged that the USAF's unilateral action not only adversely affected the scope and content of the national program but rendered the committee ineffective. At this point, GMC's Executive Director later related, the USAF representatives presented the program changes and "blandly stated that they had indeed taken this action and were so informing the Committee." The chairman reiterated his charges more strongly at the next GMG meeting, on 17 June. The matter was finally settled by the adoption of a policy statement requiring prior GMC approval of any future program change. The service subsequently honored or ignored the policy as they deemed fit. [21]

The USAF program realignment had galled GMC for several additional reasons. GMC had previously termed one of the affected projects as "sound technical planning" and another as "a valuable undertaking," but the Air Force had apparently dismissed these expert opinions. GMC also charged that another USAF change had caused a major gap in the national program--in the area of long-range (over 150 miles) ballistic missiles. To rectify this serious breach, GMC established an ad hoc subcommittee which subsequently

Filling the Gap; The Army's Corporal Missile
Source: U.S. Army

recommended that the Army develop a 500-mile ballistic missile as a follow-on to its 150-mile version and that the Air Force sponsor a study with Rand Corporation for rockets with ranges beyond 500 miles. GMC approved these recommendations in September 1948, in effect permitting the Army to fill in part the "gap" supposedly created by the Air Force. [22]

The Air Force was not alone in ignoring GMC policies. Despite GMC recommendations on several occasions, the Navy continually refused to cancel one of two duplicating projects. The Navy also disregarded GMC policy in its efforts to obtain financial support beyond that authorized for its program. The Army failed to carry out GMC recommendations for an enlarged rocket booster development program. And both the Army and Air Force deferred action on the proposed merger of their missile flight test facilities in New Mexico. [23]

After GMC's first year, the committee's secretariat conceded that the national guided missile program "is not, in fact, a unitary integrated program. but three programs." The Air Force and Navy were developing missiles in all of the four major categories and the Army in two of the four. Projects were often outright duplications with similar military characteristics and technical objectives. The Air Force member of the RDB Secretariat, Brig. Gen. James F. Phillips, blamed the civilian members of the GMC and other RDB committees for this unsatisfactory condition. The committee's military members inevitably followed a "service line," he observed, so the civilian members should direct the various development programs and eliminate unprofitable projects. "it is no secret," Phillips asserted, "that when the chips are down on a controversial problem, the civilian committee chairman and other civilians rarely vote." Because it failed to use its inherent powers, GMC acquiesced to service violations of its recommendations and decisions and to delaying tactics. [24]

Continued controversy and dispute over the content of the national guided missile program marked GMC's second year. On 15 December 1948, General McNarney, an Air Force member of RDB, predicted that there would be less funds for fiscal year 1950 than anticipated. The other board members readily agreed with him that each RDB committee review its program to eliminate all nonessential work. Accordingly, the RDB chairman on 25 January 1949 directed GMC to make an exhaustive review of all guided missile projects. He suggested that money saved from cancellations and adjustments could be used to provide more adequate support for the more essential portions of the overall program. On 10 February, GMC created an ad hoc subcommittee composed of six members, two from each service, to analyze each service's program in detail. [25]

The subcommittee deliberately avoided questioning the validity of the requirements stated by each service but tried to determine how they could be best met under the financial limitations. The Air Force offered to cancel two of its most advanced weapons, the Gapa air defense and the Matador close support missiles. The Army reluctantly offered to cancel its planned long-range surface-to-surface missile (over 500 miles) and depend on the Air Force to fill Army requirements. The Navy offered to cancel its long-range surface-to-surface missile (over 2,000 miles) and rely on the Air Force (or the Army) to develop such a weapon for use in Navy collateral functions. One Air Force officer sardonically viewed the Navy long-range missile as a project that "before these meetings did not exist" Efforts to persuade the Navy to cancel any of its three duplicating air – to - air missile projects were unsuccessful. The subcommittee accepted these offers and recommended approval by GMC. [26]

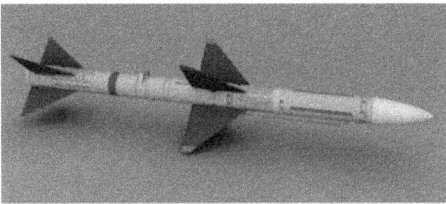

The Three Navy Missiles

The three Navy missiles referred to in the section above are shown on the left. At the top is the AAM-N-2 semi-active radar homing missile that eventually became the initially-troubled but eventually successful AIM-7 Sparrow. In the middle is the AAM-N-7 infra-red homing missile that became the phenomenally successful AIM-9 Sidewinder. The missile at the bottom is the AAM-N-4 Oriole active radar homing missile. Although the Oriole was cancelled, the technology developed for it was eventually fielded in the AIM-120 AMRAAM missile.

Source for all three pictures: U.S. Navy.

The Air Force was not too displeased with the subcommittee's recommendations, for, most importantly, they implied recognition of USAF "cognizance" over "strategic" missiles. Somewhat in the form of payment, the Air Force would give up development of Gapa and Matador. Their demise was unfortunate but unavoidable under current financial restrictions, and, in any event, the Army and Navy were developing missiles which the Air Force could use for its air defense and close support functions. [27]

The Navy's Regulus I Missile, A Close Equivalent To Matador
Source: U.S. Navy

After reviewing the subcommittee's recommendations, GMC's TEG proposed several changes. It wanted to continue Gapa and merge Matador with Regulus, a similar Navy missile. It also suggested canceling Firebird, the Air Force's only fighter-launched air-to-air missile, because of questionable technical and tactical features, the Navy project which GMC had earlier recommended be discontinued, and one of the three Navy air-to-air missiles. The Air Staff was willing to accept these changes even though funding Gapa would be a major problem. On 14 April 1949, GMC approved the subcommittee report and TEG amendments with one major exception. It believed that, despite a shortage of funds, from a technical standpoint it was premature to consolidate the Army and Navy long-range missile projects with the Air Force. [28]

The Air Force members of the RDB promptly asked the board to reverse this action. They emphasized the tremendous cost of financing the three long-range surface-to-surface missile projects. They also argued that establishment of the joint project would help refute the charges of service bickering and lack of cooperation, eliminate unwarranted and wasteful duplication, and reflect the "true spirit" and "intent" of unification. And consolidation would be in consonance with the wishes of the RDB as expressed in its letter of. 25 January 1949. But the RDB on 5 May rejected the USAF appeal and approved GMC's recommendations. In summary, this meant canceling one Air Force and two Navy projects, consolidating an Air Force and Navy project, and eliminating several research test vehicles from the national program. [29] The Navy projects included the missile (one of two Lark projects) which GMC had long wanted canceled and an in-house development that conveniently reappeared several years later. The terminated USAF project was Ryan's Firebird fighter-launched air-to-air missile. The USAF project slated for consolidation with its Navy counterpart (Regulus) was the Martin Matador. After several months of study, the Navy concluded that consolidation was inadvisable and GMC approved. Eventually, the Korean conflict engendered renewed Air Force interest in the Matador. An interesting sidelight was the rejection of the Air Force proposal to use MMK-774 Hiroc, canceled in mid-1947 as a weapon project, as a high-altitude research test vehicle. MX-774 was the direct antecedent of Atlas.

The Air Force Missile Program, 1947-1949

At the beginning of unification, the Air Force missile program included 15 projects, of which 7 were in development status, 4 were follow-on projects awaiting advances in the state of the art, 2 were study projects, and 2 (Banshee and Tarzon) were continuations of World War II projects. About this time the Air Force re-instituted a subsonic version (Snark) of one of the seven active projects and pushed the supersonic version (Boojum) into the follow-on group.

Early in 1948, the guided missile program came under the scrutiny of the USAF Aircraft and Weapons Board. The board quickly approved a new set of 13 military characteristics statements, all but one of which the Air Staff had prepared late in 1947 to replace those issued during the summer of 1945. The Air Staff spokesman, General Richardson, conceded the documents still contained "rather futuristic visionary characteristics, as aiming points to shoot at." The board also approved the initial postwar programming of production funds for the purchase of tactical, service-test, and training missiles. The amounts were rather modest -- $13 million for fiscal year 1948 and $10.3 million for the following year. This planned procurement called for a variety of items including the purchase of Razon, Tarzon, drone B-29s and F-80s, air-launching kits for the JB-2, and Q-1 drones in addition to the purchase of service test and training versions of the Martin Matador, the Ryan Firebird, and the Boeing Gapa. Much of the buying program was subsequently eliminated and substitutions made.

The Aircraft and Weapons Board paid most attention to future missile development. An AMC presentation covering the next five years revealed that inadequate funding was still the major difficulty. While approximately $33 million ($20 million for development and $13 million for production) was available for fiscal year 1948, only about $17 million ($7 million for development and $10 million for production) was anticipated for the next year. With these dreary prospects, AMC recommended canceling or reducing to component status all but 4 of the 16 study, development, and follow-on projects and upgrading of another from component to missile development status. These five development projects would meet only minimum requirements for the four categories of missiles.

Air Staff representatives counseled against accepting the AMC recommendations. There would be little or no study or development on ramjet and rocket propulsion, air defense missiles (against supersonic targets), and ballistic missiles. Work on several missiles in the advanced development state would be abandoned or sharply reduced. Nevertheless, the Aircraft and Weapons Board, and subsequently the Chief of Staff, approved AMC's recommendations although several projects would be retained if more money became available. Additional readjustments in program objectives and funds resulted in March 1948, in a program of seven development, one study, four follow-on, and two wartime carry-over projects. Although the reconstituted program showed a net loss of only one study project, realignment of program and project objectives was considerable. [30]

The Board of Senior Officers, which replaced the Aircraft and Weapons Board, again reviewed the missile program late in 1948 and early in 1949. AMC proposed no significant changes for fiscal year 1950, but the board withheld judgment on the program until funding prospects became clearer. The subsequent OSD budgetary review between January and May 1949 involving the three services and RDB and its GMC largely dictated Air Force program realignments. As a result, at the beginning of fiscal year 1950, the program included only five development, one study, four follow-on and the ever-present pair of wartime carry-over projects. Two development projects (Ryan's Firebird and Martin's Matador) were dropped. [31]

Despite periodic cutbacks, the "hardware" portion of the guided missile program showed slow but steady progress, and a gradually increasing number of vehicles were flight tested. The Air Force also contracted for several production planning studies, preparatory to authorizing missile production. And the Guided Missiles Group, DCS/Operations, noting optimistically that several USAF missiles currently carried standardization dates in 1951, recommended that they be included in Plan 52, the war plan which assumed a war-starting date of 1 July 1952.

AIR FORCE GUIDED MISSILE PROGRAM MARCH 1948

Project	Contractor	Performance	Features
Surface-to-Surface			
MX-770	North American	5,000 miles	Navaho; changed from 500 mile range winged rocket to 1,000 mile range test vehicle. To be followed by 3,000 mile range test vehicle and a 5,000 mile range operational missile. Rockets dropped for cruise propulsion
MX-771A	Glenn L Martin	500 miles	Matador Subsonic turbojet
MX-775B	Northrop	5,000 miles	Snark, subsonic turbojet, to be followed by Boojum supersonic version
MX-767	AMC	Banshee - modification of B-29 to drone	
Air-to Surface			
MX-674	Bell		Tarzon vertical bomb controllable in

			range and azimuth
MX-776	Bell	300 miles	Shrike test vehicle (and possible 50-mile range operational missile) followed by Rascal
Surface-to-air			
MX-606	Boeing	35 miles; 60,000 feet	Gapa anti-aircraft missile
MX-794	Michigan Univ	550 miles; 500,000 feet	Wizard prolonged study for anti-ballistic missile weapon.
Air-to-Air			
MX-799	Ryan	Fighter-launched	Firebird, subsonic
MX-904	Hughes	Bomber-launched	Falcon, supersonic. Upgraded from guidance component development

Ryan AAM-A-1 Firebird air-to-air missile. Firebird proved to be reasonably successful in testing but its command-guidance system limited it to clear-weather, daytime use only causing it to be cancelled in 1949

Source: U.S. Air Force

Hughes AAM-A-2 Falcon entered service in 1956 as the AIM-4 and existed in infra-red and radar homing versions

Source: U.S. Air Force

AIR FORCE GUIDED MISSILE PROGRAM JULY 1949

Project	Contractor	Performance	Features
Surface-to-Surface			
MX-770	North American	5,000 miles	Navaho; 1,000 mile range test vehicle to be followed by 3,000 mile range and a 5,000 mile range operational missiles.
MX-775B	Northrop	5,000 miles	Snark, subsonic turbojet, to be followed by Boojum supersonic version
MX-767	AMC	Banshee - modification of B-29 to drone	

Air-to Surface			
MX-674	Bell		Tarzon vertical bomb controllable in range and azimuth
MX-776	Bell	300 miles	Shrike test vehicle (and possible 50-mile range operational missile) followed by Rascal
Surface-to-air			
MX-606	Boeing	35 miles; 60,000 feet	Gapa anti-aircraft missile
MX-794	Michigan Univ	550 miles; 500,000 feet	Wizard prolonged study for anti-ballistic missile weapon.
Air-to-Air			
MX-904	Hughes	Bomber-launched	Falcon, supersonic. Upgraded from guidance component development

The Bell Aircraft ASM-A-2 Rascal air-to-surface missile. Although reasonably successful in technical terms, the rapid advance in missile technology during the 1950s made Rascal obsolete before it was deployed and the missile was cancelled in 1958

Source: U.S. Air Force

VI. THE JOHNSON ERA

In March 1949, Louis A. Johnson succeeded Forrestal as Secretary of Defense. This appointment signaled the beginning of another round of reductions in defense spending and a deepening of the conflicts among the military services over missions, roles, and funds. Johnson's avowed aim was "more unification" and more "defense per dollar." In August, Congress supported him by passing new legislation that enhanced his authority and control over the realigned and newly designated Department of Defense (DoD).

The year 1949 was highlighted by several events with far-reaching implications. The Russians continued their blockade of Berlin, intensifying the "cold war." The Western powers created the North Atlantic Treaty Organization (NATO), placing new demands upon the minimal and inadequately equipped American military forces. And the Soviet Union successfully detonated an atomic device. The basic source of American military

The U.S.S.R.'s first nuclear test
Source: U.S. Air Force

superiority was the monopoly of the atomic bomb and a marginal capability to deliver it anywhere in the world. Now, several years in advance of the best official estimates, the Russians had joined the United States as an atomic nation.

The major internal problems facing the military services at this time stemmed, as they had since the end of World War II, from inadequate funds. This inadequacy was aggravated by the practice of dividing the appropriations into three equal shares. At the bottom of virtually all disputes over missions and roles, conflicting requirement statements, and weapon claims lay the bugaboo of money. Each service emphasized its own concepts of warfare, pushed its own requirements ceaselessly, and undermined those of its sister services – all in the hope of obtaining a larger share of the slim budget. The B-36 hearings brought these inter-service dissensions dramatically into the open. The crux of the B-36 dispute was not the charge of dishonest procurement or the question of the capability of the aircraft to do its job. Concealed in the background and brought to light were questions of missions and roles, continued USAF monopoly of atomic-bomb delivery capabilities, and struggles for increased shares of defense appropriations.

These inter-service disputes obviously affected the so-called national guided missile program. They became more acute as missiles slowly progressed toward operational status. Faced with inadequate funds and ever-increasing "hardware" costs, each service promoted its own projects at the expense of the other services. The assignment of development and operational responsibilities and the priority accorded individual missiles assumed new importance. The place of each in mobilization and production planning came to be of utmost interest. The feasibility of employing atomic warheads became more than just a technical problem. The services expected to get returns from favorable decisions in these problem areas that would far exceed the boundaries of the missile field. At stake were increased financial support, enlarged roles and functions, and greater participation in any future atomic war.

Gordon Gray
Source: U.S. Army

The first missile dispute reached Secretary Johnson shortly after he assumed office, In March 1949, the Army circulated revised military characteristics statements for missiles. The Air Force took exception to several of these statements, charging that the Army wanted control over all surface-launched missiles in violation of the Army-Air Force agreements of 1947 and the Key West Agreement of March 1948. The Army retaliated in what appeared to be a once-and-for-all attempt to settle the issue. On 16 May 1949, Acting Secretary of the Army Gordon Gray asked Johnson to assign development and operational responsibility for surface-launched missiles to the Army, ship-launched missiles to the Navy, and air-launched missiles to the Air Force. [1]

Gray said that the National Security Act of. 1947 gave the Army general responsibility for "combat incident to operations on land" and that the Key West Agreement gave the Army primary interest in all land operations. Reiterating the Army's long-standing position that surface-to-air missiles were antiaircraft artillery, surface-to-surface missiles an extension of conventional artillery, and both "land combat" weapons, Gray concluded that development and operational responsibility for them should be assigned to the Army. [2]

As Gray suggested, Johnson on 25 May asked the RDB and JCS to prepare separate but coordinated replies in the light of their respective responsibilities. RDB elected to await JCS action on the operational question before dealing with the development problem. JCS assigned its task to the Joint Strategic Plans Committee (JSPC) which, in turn, gave the job to the Joint Strategic Plane Group (JSPG). [3] JSPC was a committee of representatives from the services which met as required to advise JCS while JSPG was a group of officers from the services with duty assignments in the Joint Staff.

JCS Efforts to Resolve Operational Responsibilities

Army and Navy members of the JSPG quickly found common ground and allied themselves against the Air Force representative in their deliberations on the problem of operational responsibility. On 22 July, after more than seven weeks, the group conceded that it could produce only a split report. In the interval, two other matters arose that beclouded the basic issue. The Army asked JCS to approve a high priority development project for an atomic-warhead missile and RDB submitted to JCS its annual guided missile report and stated the need for JCS strategic guidance on development priorities. [4]

The Army-Navy alliance in JSPG took the position that immediate assignment of operational responsibilities was needed to permit study of logistics, training, and operational problems concurrently with missile development. This would insure economy, reduce delays in obtaining personnel and facilities, and prevent duplicating programs and "assumed missions" from becoming entrenched in each service. The Army-Navy members of the JSPG proposed that the Air Force and Navy develop and operate air-launched missiles, the Navy ship-launched and underwater missiles, and the Army surface-launched missiles except surface-to-surface "pilot-less aircraft". The rationale, of course, was that surface-to-surface and surface-to-air missiles were merely extensions of conventional antiaircraft and field artillery.

There were several obvious obstacles to acceptance of these proposals which the Army-Navy members attempted to remove. Since the Army-Air Force agreements of 1947 had acknowledged that the Air Force was responsible for surface-launched strategic missiles, they pointed to Forestay's statement of 14 October 1947 in which he'd approved the agreements but had added that they were not final and were subject to adjustment. Now, apparently, was the time for adjustment. Again, the Key West Agreement had assigned the "air defense of the nation" mission to the Air Force, but under the Army-Navy proposal, the Air Force could neither develop nor operate surface-to-air missiles. To circumvent this contradiction, the Army-Navy members explained that although the Army would develop the missiles and organize and train units to operate them, the units employed in area defense would be placed under USAF operational "control", as provided for in the Spaatz-Devers agreement of July 1947 on antiaircraft artillery. [5]

The USAF representative on the JSPG challenged these views. Observing that very few missiles were approaching operational status, he argued that it was premature to make operational assignments. He alluded to recent efforts by RDB and its Guided Missiles Committee to achieve economy and avoid duplication of projects. He also referred to several JCS documents that allegedly provided adequate strategic guidance for missile development. The record of RDB and GMC in settling missile problems obviously did not support this favorable construction placed on their achievements. And, in view of previous USAF efforts to secure for itself uncontested assignments for missile development and operational responsibility, this argument was surprising. It could be explained, perhaps, by the strident controversy raging over the B-36 which temporarily placed the Air Force on the defensive. As prospects of winning the "head-on" missile clash with its rivals were not promising, the Air Force apparently deemed it best to deflect, if possible, the concerted Army-Navy drive. On 22 July, the day JSPG completed its split report, the Air Staff moved to take the issue out of JCS and have the War Council consider it as part of a general discussion of all new weapon systems. [6]

Brig. Gen. Joseph Smith had made his reputation with the Berlin airlift.
Source: U.S. Air Force

When JSPC received the JSPG report on 8 August 1949, its USAF member, Brig. Gen. Joseph Smith, immediately disagreed with both the Army-Navy and the Air Force positions. He did not detail his objections but commented that further discussion would be fruitless until the services agreed on the exact definition of the term "operational responsibility." Did it mean "operational control" or "operational command" or did each term have a different meaning? This question was highly germane in view of the Army-Navy interpretation of "operational responsibility." Other JSPC members agreed with General Smith on the need for more precise definitions. On 18 August, JSPC returned the split report to JSPG for reworking. [7]

Work on the main issue of responsibility made little progress while JSPG engaged in a semantical exercise. It could not agree on any of six definitions of "operational responsibility" that were advanced. In one instance, the Navy representatives could not even agree among themselves. The crux of the problem appeared to be whether the diverse Army-Navy and Air Force points of view would permit them to agree that "operational responsibility" and "operational control" had essentially identical meanings. [8]

Meanwhile, Secretary of the Air Force Symington on 19 August sent Secretary Johnson the proposal which the Air Staff had prepared on 22 July as an alternative for settling the operational responsibility issue. The proposal was, in fact, the same as the one which the Air Staff in July 1948 had suggested that Symington send to Forrestal in order to thwart the Army's informal proposal for a joint Army-Air Force review of existing operational assignments. [9]

Symington indicated that the fundamental consideration in assigning operational responsibility for any weapon should be its effectiveness and economy in meeting defense requirements. The fact that one service developed a weapon was not particularly pertinent. Operational assignments should depend on service missions and roles and a JCS determination that a service required the weapon. This policy should not be confined to guided missiles but should include atomic, biological, radiological, and other new weapons". [10]

On 1 September 1949, JCS discussed the Symington proposal and informally agreed to recommend its adoption by the Armed Forces Policy Council (AFPC) that had replaced the War Council as part of the revision to the National Security Act of 1947. But on 20 September, Gray opposed it within the council and the Army and Navy service chiefs asked for a delay until JCS could prepare a formal position. Johnson now solicited the views of JCS on the proposal, and that body asked JSPC to review it in conjunction with the spit JSPG report. JSPC replied that "no agreement on basic issues could be reached".

On 26 September, the day before the next scheduled JCS discussion on the Gray and Symington proposals, General Smith circulated within JSPC a revised USAF position on the issue of missile operational responsibility. Long in preparation and carefully coordinated by all sections of the Air Staff, it differed markedly from the Air Force position in the original JSPG report. Its completion and circulation was adroitly handled to permit the Army and Navy only limited time in which to prepare counter-arguments". [12]

Smith emphasized the major points of the Symington proposal. Responsibility for or control over weapons flowed directly from assigned service functions. JCS should decide operational requirements for each missile and only on the basis of service functions, no matter the developing agency. It should assign individual missiles, not broad categories, but not before the developer and RDB reported proved weapon characteristics and capabilities. Smith pointed out that the Gray proposal would give a service exclusive responsibility over broad categories of missiles and create, in effect, "a future function for a service by predetermination of control over a weapon, instead of deriving that control from presently agreed functions." Perhaps more significantly, it contradicted the existing procedure of stating functions in terms of service activity and then establishing requirements and developing weapons to support the functions". [13]

There were immediate gestures of compromise by both the Army and the Air Force. Correctly sensing that the Air Force was most concerned about losing its strategic bombardment function, the Army's JSPC representative proposed that JCS defer assignment of long-range missiles because there was inadequate data on their performance. A few days later, the Air Force's Chief of Staff, General Vandenberg, indicated that at the next JCS meeting he would concede to the Army the use of surface-to-air missiles for local (point) defense and of surface-to-surface missiles for close ground support. But the Air Force expected to retain operational responsibility for missiles employed for general (area) defense, for strategic bombardment, and for missiles which replaced fighter aircraft. [14]

When JCS convened on 29 September, it faced a 119-page report on missile operational responsibility that contained the original Army-Navy and Air Force positions prepared in JSPG, the newly revised Air Force position, and the Army's compromise proposal to defer consideration of responsibility for long-range strategic missiles. In order to analyze fully these wide divergences,

JCS accepted the advice of its Operations Deputies (Generals Lauris Norstad, Alfred Gruenther, and Admiral A. D. Struble for the Air Force, Army, and Navy, respectively) who were senior officers, one from each service. They met prior to a JCS meeting to clarify and settle as many agenda items as possible to relieve JCS of its workload. Unanimous decisions of the Operations Deputies were usually ratified by JCS. The deputies promised to assist JSPC in preparing a reply to the Secretary of Defense on the points raised by the Gray and Symington memorandums. Meanwhile, Johnson agreed to extend the deadline for settling the issue from 4 October to 15 November. [15]

Despite the guidance of the Operations Deputies, JSPG and JSPC were unable to resolve the conflicting views. As the deadline neared, the deputies took matters into their own hands and on 31 October drafted a reply which largely avoided the main issues. It stated that JCS could recommend operational assignments for some, but not all, categories of guided missiles and would therefore soon make recommendations on surface-to-air and short-range surface-to-surface missiles. Slightly altering the Symington proposal, it suggested that all weapons, no matter the developing agency, would be available to any service in the discharge of assigned functions. The important change was that the individual services, not JCS, would determine requirements for a specific missile, and JCS could only approve or disapprove. [16]

The Army's Chief of Staff, Gen. J. Lawton Collins, was dissatisfied with this draft, but he was apparently willing to forego some of the Army's original demands. The Operations Deputies therefore redrafted their reply to state that development had progressed to the point where proper operational assignments were "recognizable" in most categories of missiles. They recommended the following: surface-to-air missiles which extended the range of antiaircraft artillery to the Army and Navy, surface-to-air missiles which supplemented interceptor aircraft to the Air Force and Navy, short-range surface-to-surface missiles used in place of field artillery and naval guns to the Army and Navy, and air-launched missiles to the Air Force and Navy. The Marine Corps could employ any missile required in carrying out its functions. There was also a change to the broad policy statement: all service determinations on weapon requirements were to be honored "subject to final approval of the Joint Chiefs of Staff on the basis of its contribution to the overall war effort in any case where conflicts of functions or economy may arise." In effect, JCS would become involved only after one service challenged the need of another for a particular missile or because of financial considerations. [17]

JCS approved this draft on 17 November 1949 and sent it to Johnson. The AFPC also approved it, at a 6 December meeting. However, Johnson withheld comment on the JCS recommendations until he received RDB's proposals on missile development assignments and results of an interdepartmental review of the guided missile programs. These caused an unexpected delay, and he made no decision until 21 March 1950. [18]

In summary, after six months of debate, the JCS reply to Johnson contained nothing that altered the functions each service believed it possessed before 16 May 1949. Nor did it transfer missiles to carry out those functions. JCS omitted recommendations on surface-launched long-range missiles but so long as the Air Force retained the strategic bombardment function it would be their logical user when they became operational. The Air Force regarded as a major victory the JCS acknowledgement that possession (development) of a weapon did not in itself allow acquisition of a function. In the view of some Air Staff officials, the Air Force had successfully repelled the Army's "carefully calculated effort to change the Functions Paper by obtaining responsibilities which would in effect give absolute control over all strategic warfare launched from "terra firma""[19]

RDB-GMC Efforts to Resolve Development Responsibilities

Secretary Johnson on 25 May 1949 had asked JCS and RDB to reply to the Gray proposal and resolve the issues of missile operational and development assignments. GMC's executive director immediately suggested that Johnson be informed that existing development assignments were satisfactory. Instead, RDB on 2 June asked for a deferment until JCS decided the operational issues. The board promised to assist JCS and offered the services of an ad hoc sub-committee. [20]

After JCS on 17 November forwarded its recommendations, the GMC secretariat listed all missile development projects and found them with one exception to be in consonance with JCS-proposed operational responsibilities. The exception was USAF's Gapa air defense missile, which was already in the process of being canceled. These findings were surprising, for JCS had deliberately not defined the distinction between surface-to-air missiles which replaced anti-aircraft artillery and interceptor aircraft and the dividing line (in miles) between short- and long- range surface -to - surface missiles. And JCS had made no recommendations on long-range missiles. [21]

On 15 December, GMC formally noted the JCS recommendations, the findings of its own staff, and decided to take no further action. But the RDB asked GMC to complete the job which Johnson had directed in May. GMC reacted by establishing an ad-hoc sub-committee, consisting of one representative from each service, which reported a short time later that it could not act until the high-level Special Interdepartmental Board (commonly known as the Stuart Board) reviewed the national missile program. Once again, GMC put aside the issue of development assignments. [22]

After Secretary Johnson in mid-March 1950 approved most of the Stuart Board and JCS recommendations, GMC's ad hoc subcommittee again took up the question of development responsibilities. In its report of 31 March, it observed that each service could adequately carry out its missile projects "in terms of technical personnel, facilities and workloads," inter-service coordination was excellent and no change in development assignments was necessary or desirable. [23]

Meanwhile, the GMC secretariat (comprised of civilians), sensing continued OSD dissatisfaction with the guided missile program, had proposed a radical alternative. It suggested that an entire category of projects (surface-to-surface, surface-to-air, etc), no matter the developing agency, be assigned to the coordinative supervision of a single service. Although each service would continue its own projects, the designated service would coordinate all projects within the category. Disputes could be appealed to GMC.

GMC took up both sets of recommendations on 24 April and accepted those of its sub-committee. These were sent to RDB, together with a list showing all missile development projects of each service conveniently matched to the recently approved operational assignments. RDB also had to weigh conflicting recommendations, for its secretariat had espoused the proposal of the GMC secretariat and suggested a study on the assignment of the entire missile program (or major categories thereof) to a single service. The RDB on 17 May rejected the alternative plan, endorsed GMC's recommendations, and sent its views to Johnson on 9 June 1950, 13 months after he had asked for them. The board stated that it intended to make development assignments generally along the lines established by JCS for operational missile responsibilities. This would account for about 70 percent of the national missile effort. The remainder involved development of components, an area RDB intended to study further before making recommendations. [25]

Johnson found this position unacceptable because JCS operational assignments were too broad to serve as a guide for determining development assignments. While one, two, or three services might have legitimate operational requirements for a missile, he said, not all should attempt to develop it. Since a service could easily interpret the RDB policy as authority to duplicate a project, Johnson asked how the board would prevent duplication and assure economy of funds and effort. [26]

Early in August 1950, RDB replied that it was reviewing its policies on all weapon development assignments, not missiles alone and would not make further recommendations on missile development assignments until completing the review. Thus, this knotty problem was again quiescent, a condition the three services benignly accepted. After five years, the problem of missile development assignments was still unresolved. [27]

DOD Missile Program Review

The Gray and Symington proposals of May and August 1949 had caused an intensive examination of missile development and operational responsibilities, but they had not in themselves effected a reduction in the size of the guided missile programs, although this was a logical possibility. However, Secretary Johnson, interested in additional defense economies and influenced by legislation of May 1949 authorizing but not appropriating $75 million for a long-range proving ground in Florida, called for an examination of the missile program. On 15 July 1949, he asked RDB to report on the program, particularly on the status of current and planned facilities, development assignments, and project duplication. [28]

Dr. Karl T. Compton, the RDB chairman, turned to GMC for information and advice, and the committee furnished a number of stock generalities for use in countering Johnson's obvious intentions. Missiles would revolutionize the concepts of war, their increased war capability easily justified current expenditures, and the development program was unique both in difficulty and cost because there was usually only one flight per test missile. GMC also asserted that the missile program had been funded at arbitrarily low levels during the last three years despite rising "hardware" costs and inflation, and further cuts could lead only to undesirable program gaps and unfulfilled military requirements. [29]

Dr. Karl T. Compton
Source: Massachusetts
Institute of Technology

Before Compton could prepare his reply, Johnson called for another general reduction in the slim fiscal year 1950 budget. RDB turned to its committees for suggestions on where to apply the reductions. Dr. Clark B. Millikan, GMC's chairman, observed that the services were reviewing their budgets and that it was not the job of his committee to judge the validity of service requirements and then determine where to reduce. "Moreover," he added "GMC had already reviewed the budget three times and proposed cuts well below the safe minimum. [30]

Meanwhile, the RDB executive director had suggested that those missile projects in jurisdictional dispute along the services be considered for cancellation if reductions were directed. Although Millikan deplored this idea as a suitable basis for making budget cuts, the executive director of his committee on the same day sent RDB a "Staff Analysis of Controversial Guided Missile items." The proposal was indeed based on a fallacy since the dispute over responsibility for air defense or long-range surface-to-surface missiles in no way invalidated or lowered the priority of their requirement. [31]

RDB on 26 October 1949 considered the various committee reports and staff studies and decided that only $15 million (of which $1 million was for missiles) could be squeezed from the development budget. Because this reduction was so small, DoD's Management Committee termed the RDB report an unsatisfactory response to Johnson's request. [32]

Discouraged with missile budgetary prospects, Dr. Compton decided to make a stand against further cuts. On 31 October, in an interim Program review report to Johnson, he emphasized the unique capabilities of missiles for replacing aircraft, anti-aircraft and field artillery. The three military department heads, with Secretary Symington as chairman, carried out a project-by-project review and prepared a joint program that would be economical and also effectively managed. Symington then proposed that a special board do the work, a step that Johnson approved on 20 December. The new board, officially the Special Interdepartmental Guided Missiles Board (also SIGMB, SIB, and the Stuart Board after Harold C. Stuart, its chairman), consisted of one under or assistant secretary from each department, the RDB chairman and a working group of one senior officer from each service. [35]

Harold C. Stuart
Source: U.S. Air Force

The board consisted of Harold C. Stuart, Assistant Secretary of the Air Force; Dan A. Kimball, Under Secretary of the Navy; Archibald S. Alexander, Assistant Secretary of the Army; and Robert F. Rinehart, Acting Chairman of the RDB. Although it had a reporting deadline of 15 January L950, the Stuart Board met 11 times between 21 December and 1 February and did not submit its findings until early in February. The Stuart Board concentrated on three major topics: possible consolidation, reorientation, or cancellation of projects; operation of missile ranges; and inauguration of personnel training and procurement (production) funding. As expected, the issues of "dollars" and operational responsibility became the major points of contention and led to heated discussions, generally with the Air Force at odds with the Army, Navy, and RDB. To Johnson, a prime reason for reviewing the missile program was to reduce costs during fiscal year l950 and subsequent years.

Some Air Force participants, alarmed that the Stuart Board and Johnson might agree with the Navy charges and that the Air Force as a result might lose the strategic function, considered asking JCS for long-range missile operational responsibility and higher priority ratings. Other Air Staff officers opposed exerting pressure on JCS lest the Air Force forfeit all claim to short- and medium-range missiles as the price of obtaining long-range responsibility. They believed that time was still on the side of the Air Force and there was little chance of the Navy forcing cancellation of the USAF projects. [38] Although the Air Force did not press the matter, JCS nevertheless soon became embroiled in this operational question as a result of the Stuart Board findings.

By the end of January 1950, the Stuart Board had completed its report. It was a complex document, containing a list of agreements and disagreements, three statements on service views plus one on the RDB's position, and two policy drafts on operating test ranges and improving procedures for coordinating and controlling the program. Of the individual weapon, study, and test vehicle projects reviews, the 4 participating agencies agreed to continue 14 (3 Air Force, 5 Army, and 6 Navy). Additionally, 10 projects (4 Army and 6 Navy) received the support of 3 participants, with the Air Force non-concurring on all of them. Finally, two or more participants questioned some aspect of or suggested a major orientation to three projects, all Air Force sponsored [39]

The Army's Requirement for a defensive missile capable of destroying enemy supersonic missiles eventually became the MIM-23 HAWK.

Source: U.S. Army

The Army's statement of views included a call for an energetic effort to develop a defensive missile capable of destroying enemy supersonic missiles. The RDB should examine the status of surface-to-surface missiles with ranges over 500 miles and recommend the service to develop them. JCS should review the requirement for Navaho in the light of its expected high cost. In any case, this missile should not have a priority rating equal to missiles with ranges under 1,000 miles. [40]

The Navy's statement was essentially an attack against the Air Force missile program. After claiming that its own was "technically sound, practical, and economical" and the Army's "conservative and practical," the Navy charged that the Air Force's was "out of balance." On the basis of JCS priority guidance, the Navy said, the Air Force had "overstressed long-range missile development at the expense of air defense missiles". Pointing to the fiscal year

1950 budget, the Navy observed that it had allocated 20 percent and the Army 50 percent of their respective missile development funds for air defense missiles (surface-to-air and air-to-air) in accordance with JCS-recommended priorities. By contrast, the Air Force had earmarked only 22 percent for air defense missiles and about 64 percent for the lower-rated long-range surface-to-surface missiles.

The Navy also maintained that the requirement for the Florida missile range, while necessary was not urgent. It should be financed by USAF withdrawal from the operation of the Holloman, New Mexico, range and by "a realistically organized program in the very long-range surface-to-surface missiles." Otherwise, other projects would suffer from inadequate financing. The Navy also defended its projects against charges of duplication, urged the joint use of ranges, and stressed the need to determine operational responsibility over long-range missiles. In summary, the Navy appeared intent on restricting Air Force development of long-range surface-to-surface missiles until it could claim a part of the strategic function. [41]

The Air Force position was brief and to the point. To economize and to eliminate duplication, a service should develop only one missile in any category (surface-to-air, air-to-air, etc) in which it had operational responsibility. This policy would reduce the national missile program to 13 weapon system projects. Funds obtained from the terminated projects would be applied to those remaining. Perhaps not unintentionally this proposal would also strike at the heart of the Navy development concept of supporting several duplicating projects at once, each with a different technical approach, to obtain a single objective. [42]

The RDB statement was quite innocuous. It advocated retention of a substantial program of subsystem and component research and development. It also urged that funds recovered from project terminations be reallocated to the rest of the missile programs.[43]

The Stuart Board unanimously agreed on two major recommendations: operation of a range by each service but jointly used and establishment of an interdepartmental operational requirements group for guided missiles. This group would largely coordinate such matters as operational requirements, military characteristics, training, and missile force-integration planning. [44]

Stuart sent the report to the three departmental secretaries on 3 February 1950, and each appended comments. Secretary of the Army Gray reaffirmed the Army views, disagreed with the Air Force proposal to limit development to one project in each operational category, and urged continuation of all projects approved by three of the four Stuart Board members. He also advised against JCS making recommendations on long-range missile operational assignments at this time, completely reversing his position of 16 May 1949. Secretary of the Navy Francis P. Matthews supported the position taken by the Navy's board representative and also disagreed with the Air Force's proposal of one project per operational category.

Secretary Symington submitted the most detailed comments. He noted that among the 20-odd projects, there were frequently 2 or 3 and, in one instance, 5 missiles being developed to do the same job. While there had been ample reason in the past for duplication in order to investigate various technical approaches, this practice had not produced the desired. exchange of information among interested companies and services and was no longer warranted. Since the Soviet Union had developed the atomic bomb and means to deliver it and had a crash missile development program under way, the American missile program had to be changed from casual research to the production of operational weapons at the earliest date.

Foreseeing little possibility of obtaining additional missile funds, Symington restated the Air Force proposal to restrict each service to no more than one project for each operational category. This would eliminate 10 projects, leave 13 (3 Air Force, 2 Army, and 8 Navy), and save about 25 percent in expenditures currently planned for the next five years. Should the DOD reject this proposal and JCS fail to recommend the assignment of strategic missiles to one service, the five long-range projects alone would consume more than one-third of the missile budget during the next five years and as much as 70 percent after 1955. [45] T.G. Lanphier, Jr. , Special Consultant to Symington, had drafted much of Symington's statement. He indicated that Generals Vandenberg and Norstad had checked the draft and thought it "extreme. " Reportedly Norstad hoped that Symington would include an "intermediate proposal" that could be used if Johnson did not cut the missile program as much as feared.

The Stuart Report and the secretarial comments went to Johnson on 9 February 1950 and were discussed by AFPC a week later. Johnson expressed dissatisfaction with both the wide divergence of opinion and the "softness", of the guided missile program. He weighed the idea suggested by the chairman of the Munitions Board, that an individual or agency outside DoD be appointed to bring order out of the program. Symington and others persuaded him, however, to try further internal action, and a JCS offer to tackle the job was accepted. [46]

After receiving a JSPG-JSPC report and briefings from the three services and the RDB, JCS on 23 February 1950 examined the major points of the Stuart Report. The service chiefs opposed the proposal that a service develop only one missile in any category in which it had operational responsibility. They settled the mode of operation for missiles ranges accepted the idea of an interdepartmental operational requirements group, and took an uncertain position on the operational employment of surface-to-surface missiles. JCS also reviewed each project and assigned it a particular status rating such as weapon development, component development, design study, or research study. Finally, JCS agreed to conduct similar reviews annually, beginning about 1 September 1950. [47]

Converting the verbal agreements to written statements acceptable to the services proved a stumbling block for almost 3 weeks. For a time, there was danger that the JCS agreement would be undone. A major point of contention dealt with surface-to-surface missiles. As stated in the original draft, the Navy and Army could develop and employ them in sea and land combat as required by assigned functions and the Air Force only as a supplement or replacement for aircraft used in strategic warfare. This theoretically allowed the Army and Navy to use all types of surface-to-surface missiles but restricted the Air Force to long-range missiles that directly supported strategic warfare. The Air staff thought that JCS should broaden the Air Force assignment to correspond to that of the other services. When Army and Navy representatives refused to change the wording, some Air Staff members wanted to accede, as it gave the Air Force missiles for strategic purposes. Others disagreed, believing that the Air Force should be allowed to use surface-to-surface missiles in meeting requirements of assigned functions in addition to strategic warfare.[48]

At one point, Army and Navy planners suggested deletion of the topic, but this would have left a most crucial point unsettled. JCS then proposed that long-range missiles be operationally assigned as required by the functions of the three services. This was still unsatisfactory to the Air Force, for it would have rights only to long-range surface-to-surface missiles while the Army and Navy could use any missile, no matter its range, so long as they justified it on the basis of assigned functions. The Air Staff then considered the idea of breaking the controversial area into short-, medium-, and long-range missiles and allowing all services to employ the first two but restricting use of the third to the Air Force. The Air Force did not submit the plan, however, believing it stood little chance of acceptance. With an approaching deadline, JCS moved to a swift resolution of the problem. On 13 March, the Operations Deputies weighed the amended version and a last minute plan advanced by the Air Force whereby JCS would relate surface-to-surface missiles to existing conventional weapons for which responsibility was already known. In this way, they would fall agreeably into four categories: those replacing field artillery or naval guns, assigned to the Army and Navy; those replacing close support aircraft, assigned to the Army and Air Force; those replacing naval aircraft, to the Navy; those replacing aircraft other than close support, to the Air Force. The next day, JCS confirmed the deputies acceptance of the plan. [50]

Another controversy developed over the duties of the interdepartmental operational requirements group which the Stuart Board had recommended. The Army and Navy wanted the group to formulate missile development and production programs while the Air Force believed that the group's proper role was to formulate requirements upon which the services would then formulate their programs -- a distinction of considerable significance. In either case, the JCS would have final approval authority. JCS finally accepted the Air Force position. [51]

The third major area of contention concerned the status ratings JCS assigned the-individual missile projects. As expected, the major difficulty involved the long- range surface-to-surface missiles. The Air Staff contended that the Army and Navy should discontinue their projects in this field because they had no functions that required such missiles. General Vandenberg chose not to pursue this approach in JCS "at this time" hoping that the gradual and orderly realignment of the development program to conform with operational requirements would eventually provide the solution. [52]

The Navy, as in the Stuart Board meetings, attacked the Air Force's long-range projects. JCS had reduced one (Snark) to development of a guidance system only and limited the other (Navaho) to "design study and development of components." The Chief of Naval Operations suggested that Snark be canceled unless Navaho required the guidance system and that Navaho be restricted to a design study. The Air Force replied that the Navy's long-range missile (Triton) should be similarly reduced. In addition, it asked permission to upgrade the Snark slightly by building "test vehicles" to evaluate the guidance system. JCS approved the Navy's position on Triton and the Air Force's on Snark and Navaho, and it consolidated Army short- and long-range missile projects. [53]

AIR FORCE GUIDED MISSILE PROGRAM JULY 1950

Project	Contractor	Performance	Features
Surface-to-Surface			
MX-770	North American	5,000 miles	Navaho; 1,000 mile air launched missile to be followed by 1,700 mile range air-launched and a 5,500 mile range surface-launched operational missiles.
MX-775B	Northrop	5,000 miles	Snark, downgraded to development of guidance subsystem and guidance test vehicle
Air-to Surface			
MX-674	Bell		Tarzon vertical bomb controllable in range and azimuth
MX-776	Bell	300 miles	Rascal 1 with 100 mile range to be followed by Rascal II with 150 mile range
Surface-to-air			
MX-1593	Boeing	100 miles; 60,000 feet	BOMARC anti-aircraft missile
MX-794	Michigan Univ	550 miles; 500,000 feet	Wizard prolonged study for anti-ballistic missile weapon.
Air-to-Air			
MX-904	Hughes	Supersonic	Falcon, fighter-launched to be followed by Bomber-launched version

On 15 March 1950, JCS sent Johnson a memorandum that contained the proposed project status ratings, approved the Stuart Board recommendations on the operation of the missile ranges and the establishment of the

interdepartmental group, and recommended that the proposed operational responsibility assignments of 17 November 1949 be amended to include the current JCS agreement on surface-to-surface missiles. Finally, JCS recommended only a small reduction in the size of the missile program. Three projects were canceled. Two were Army projects and one subsequently reappeared. The other was a Navy project. It, too, later reappeared--as an ordnance rather than as a missile item. Another missile was transferred from the Navy to the Army. There were virtually no reductions in cost. [54]

The CIM-10 Bomarc missile replaced Gapa. It would be the only surface-to-air missile ever deployed by the United States Air Force

Source: U.S. Air Force

Johnson was apparently dissatisfied with the minor cutback, for he held a special meeting on 20 March. RDB officials made a detailed presentation on all aspects of the missile development program. His concern allayed, Johnson indicated his satisfaction with the exhaustive Stuart and JCS studies and decided not to reduce the program further. He still believed that the program lacked adequate top-level control, however, and said that he would look to the interdepartmental requirements group to provide it. He asked JCS to select the members carefully and have the group report to him, through JCS, every 90 days. The next day, Johnson formally approved the JCS recommendations of 17 November 1949 and 15 March 1950. [55]

Although the Air Force would later regret several decisions of its Chief of Staff, for the moment it believed it had fared well. It had received formal recognition of its operational responsibility for both short-range tactical and long-range strategic missiles, no projects were terminated, and a reasonable solution for operating the ranges had been obtained. Mr. Lanphier, Symington's special consultant, evaluated the results as follows: "In summation, the Air Force position in the field of guided missiles is considerably improved by the JCS action in 1620/17 (the 15 March memorandum to Johnson]. Improved, that is, to the extent that the Air Force now has a legitimate basis upon which to act in the extension, with guided missiles, of all its assigned responsibilities and functions. Needless to say, the license to act is footless without continuing exercise of that license in a highly competitive and critical field of research and development."

Lanphier also expected optimistically that JCS and its operational requirements group would play positive roles in the missile program and that inter-service rivalries might end. Time would prove him wrong in both assumptions. [56]

Review of Missile Priority Ratings

Johnson's relentless drive for economy vitally affected another facet of the missile program -- priority ratings for the individual projects. As Johnson reduced budgets and planned other cuts, the services became increasingly concerned with project priorities. Projects with the highest ratings had the best chance of surviving and obtaining enough funds to allow normal development" Under ever-increasing financial pressures, the preparation. and allocation of priority ratings for missile projects became another area of contention among the services.

The problem first evolved from the annual. missile report that RDB sent to JCS on 21 July 1949. One section of the report dealt with priorities and how they were established. Each service had designated them for its own program. The Air Force, for example, placed its highest priority on missiles which enhanced the offensive and defensive capabilities of strategic bombers and gave second priority to air defense missiles. GMC's TEG consolidated these lists into one eight-point listing: [57]

Priority	Category	Nearest Conventional Equivalent
1	SAM (against aircraft and missiles)	Antiaircraft Artillery
2	AAM (fighter- and bomber-launched)	Aircraft Armament
3	ASM (against strategic targets)	Strategic Bombing
4	SSM (against strategic targets)	Strategic Bombing
5	SSM (in support of troops)	Artillery
6	ASM (against tactical targets)	Tactical Bombing
7	SUM	Antisubmarine Warfare
8	Converted aircraft (drones)	

In preparing the eight-point listing, the evaluation group also relied on broad strategic guidance that JCS had provided RDB on 5 May 1948 and subsequently amplified when the board formulated its procedures for an overall DOD research and development master plan According to this guidance, JCS wanted the development program to support objectives in six broad areas in the following order of priority:

(1) control of intervening space, especially air and underwater;

(2) strategic reduction of enemy war-making potential;

(3) intelligence and psychological warfare;

(4) land, sea, and air tactical operations;

(5) local defense;

(6) mobilization of manpower and industry. [58]

Since it intended to use the priorities in planning the fiscal year 1950 missile program, RDB asked JCS to confirm the validity of its strategic guidance and comment on the consolidated missile program priorities that TEG had outlined. [59]

During protracted JSPG discussions, the Army insisted that atomic-equipped missiles be included in the priority ratings, although JCS had not yet acted on the Army's request. After other JSPG members agreed to add the comment that the ratings might have to be changed as a result of feasibility studies under way, the Army member accepted this interim solution. On 22 August 1949, JSPG unanimously agreed that the RDB priority list was generally in accord with JCS strategic guidance. [60]

The Army representative on the JSPG challenged the report. He opposed classifying and rating missiles on the basis of "strategic" and "tactical" targets and wanted to substitute the phrases "against distant targets" and "in direct support of ground troops." He also demanded relegation of strategic surface-to-surface missiles from fourth to sixth priority, following surface- and air-launched tactical missiles. As a result, the committee returned the report to JSPG.[61]

Efforts to reconcile the conflicting views failed, and almost a month later JSPG issued a split report. Navy and Army representatives joined in devising a new priority list. Claiming that the existing list was open to misunderstanding, they placed the four broad categories of missiles in the following order of priority:

surface-to-air
air-to-air
air-to- surface
surface-to- surface.

These four categories were then broken down into 13 subcategories, as follows:

Priority   Subcategories
1   SAM vs. subsonic aircraft
2   AAM (fighter-launched)
3   SAM vs. supersonic aircraft or guided missiles
4   ASM with atomic warhead
5   SSM (short-range with atomic warhead)
6   AAM (bomber-launched)
7   ASM (HE and incendiary warheads)
8   SSM (long-range with atomic warhead)
9   ASM vs. underwater targets
10   SSM (short-range with HE and incendiary warhead)
11   SSM (long-range with HE and incendiary warheads)
12   SSM vs. underwater targets
13   Converted aircraft (drones)

The Air Force representative believed that the priority ratings for the four major categories reflected JCS guidance but the 13 subcategories did not. He proposed regrouping the surface-to-surface missiles without regard to the type of warhead. The 10 subcategories remaining would be basically in consonance with JCS strategic guidance and the ratings originally proposed by RDB and initially approved by JSPG. [62]

JSPG was unable to resolve the conflict and sent the split report to JCS, who reviewed it on 25 October 1949. The Air Force wanted JCS to postpone a decision until it first settled the question of missile operational responsibility that had been pending since May and until RDB commented on the recently completed Hull Committee report on the feasibility of combining atomic warheads with missiles. When JCS promised to reopen the question of priorities after the RDB comments became available, the Air Force vice chief of staff, Gen Muir S. Fairchild, withdrew the request for postponement and reluctantly approved the Army-Navy proposal for the 13 subcategory ratings. [63]

Many dissatisfied Air Staff officials felt that JCS had repudiated its own six-point strategic guidance. Short-range surface-to-surface missiles in support of ground troops now enjoyed a higher priority than long-range strategic missiles and bomber-launched defensive missiles, reversing the relative development priority of the tactical and strategic missiles. And the Army had apparently gained a role in the atomic-weapon field and a share of the stockpile that the Air Force still deemed inadequate for strategic bombardment purposes. The Air Staff therefore authorized a series of studies, Preparatory to asking JCS to review and revise its strategic guidance and the missile priority list after the RDB commented on the atomic warhead feasibility study. A propitious time for reopening the question failed to appear, however, even after RDB forwarded its comments. On 30 December 1949, almost in passing, JCS reaffirmed the priority ratings of 25 October as part of its call for atomic-equipped guided missiles. [64]

As earlier noted, at the conclusion of the Stuart Board and JCS missile programs review in March 1950, the RDB made a special presentation to Johnson. It disclosed that the Air Force had no first or second priority projects and only a study project in the third priority grouping. Most of the Air Force missile funds, effort, and attention was concentrated on long-range strategic missiles, far down in eighth place on the priority list. Although these facts were embarrassing, the Air Force could find no suitable way to change the priorities. The Guided Missile Interdepartmental Operational Requirements Group, established at Johnson's direction in March 1950 as advisers to JCS, would obviously be preoccupied with priorities (theoretically they reflected the urgency of operational requirements) so a direct appeal to JCS by the Air Force was unattractive. Not until the Korean conflict began in June 1950 did the priority problem lessen, when additional appropriations obviated the need to appeal the JCS missile ratings of 25 October 1949. [65]

Policies and Plans for Atomic-Equipped Missiles

Although Air Staff development officials had suggested within hours after the Hiroshima explosion the possibility of equipping guided missiles with atomic warheads, converting the proposal into fact was a complex, confusing, and frustrating experience. After more than two years of negotiating and haggling with the Manhattan District and AEC, the Air Force finally conceded its inability to carry out the proposal. A requirement for atomic warheads was included in a number of missile military characteristics statements issued during October and November 1947, but the Air Force did practically nothing about it.

Early in 1949, an AEC official conjectured that there had been enough technological progress in both atomic energy and missiles to consider seriously the development of atomic-equipped guided missiles. For its part, AEC started a feasibility study on warheads. Learning about this, an Air Staff official cautiously stated, "it seems advisable that the USAF decide whether the USAF guided missile program has advanced sufficiently to warrant atomic warhead development by the AEC." Thereafter, the Air Force examined systematically the requirements, cost, tactical worth, and other facets associated with the development of atomic-equipped missiles, hoping to have "all the facts" before approaching AEC with warhead requirements. To do otherwise, remarked one participant, "will only embarrass the USAF."

The Army and the Marines both had a requirement for a mobile, short-range, nuclear-armed battlefield support missile. This became the MGM-18 Lacrosse.

Source: U.S. Army

The Army, long looking for a means of obtaining a role in atomic warfare and breaking the Air Force monopoly on delivery moved considerably faster. On 24May 1949, about the time it proposed to assume responsibility for all surface-launched missiles, the Army asked JCS to recommend the establishment of an "urgent requirement" for a short- range surface-to-surface guided missile equipped with an atomic warhead. The Army Chief of Staff observed that the development appeared practical. He justified the requirement on the ground that the Army's additional responsibilities in Western Europe under the NATO pact would be eased immensely if the local Army commander possessed an all-weather atomic weapon in support of land operations. The NATO pact was signed on 4 April 1949 and entered into force on 24 August 1949. The Army did not mention that establishment of an "urgent requirement" would ease financing of the- project, a matter of import in that period of stringent economy and periodic budget reductions. [67]

In supporting the Army request, the Chief of Naval operations added that his service also needed the weapon. He asserted, however, that the Army's requirement should not have a priority above those for air-to-air and surface-to-air missiles. (The Navy had three missiles under development in each of the two categories.) [68]

The Air Staff labeled the Army proposal as another "piecemeal approach" to at least three distinct problems needing inter-service agreement. The first, the operation of this Army-proposed missile, was part of the overall question of missile operational responsibility facing the JCS. The second, the urgency of the missile, should not be affirmed, the Air staff believed, until JCS reviewed all current missile priority ratings. The third related to the limited atomic stockpile. The Air Force held that JCS should determine targets and the circumstances under which the services could use atomic weapons. The Army had proposed far more latitude of authority for its field commanders than it had been willing to grant Air Force and Navy commanders. [69]

During the JCS discussions, Vandenberg agreed on the need to develop atomic-equipped guided missiles but he believed that JCS should not make operational assignments except as part of the overall question before it. Nor should the new, work disturb established priorities without a JCS review of the whole missile program. He suggested that JCS first ask RDB for its views on the development of atomic-equipped missiles. If RDB found that this would materially affect the priorities of the current program, then the board should refer the matter back to JCS. On 12 July 1949, JCS accepted Vandenberg's interim solution and informed RDB two days later. [70]

Meanwhile, independent of the JCS proceedings, Johnson on the advice of his Deputy for Atomic Energy Matters had established on 21 June 1949 a three-man ad hoc committee to study the technical feasibility of combining atomic warheads with guided missiles. The members were Lt. Gen. J. E. Hull, Director of Weapons Systems Evaluation Group (Chairman); Dr. F. T. Hovde, President of Purdue University; and Dr. N. E. Bradbury, Director of the Los Alamos Scientific Laboratory. Brig. Gen. James McCormack, Jr., the Director of the Division of Military Applications, AEC, served as committee secretary. Lt. Gen. Hull, explained that his group would assess development possibilities

Lt Gen John Edwin Hull
Source: U.S. Army

over the ensuing 5 to 10 years but would not examine the question of military worth. Instead, it would pass its findings to appropriate agencies within the Defense Department, letting them determine this matter. [71]

On 20 July, RDB notified JCS that development of the new type of missile would indeed disturb current priority ratings. The board advised, however, against any shift until Hull's committee completed its study. JCS accepted this advice and also decided to await RDB's reaction to the Hull report before again taking up the Army's proposal. [72]

When RDB the next day sought JCS advice on existing missile priorities, it also reopened the question. The Army took this opportunity to obtain a suitable rating for short-range surface-to-surface missiles with atomic warheads. On 25 October 1949, JCS approved a new priority list that included missiles with atomic war-heads even though it had not yet acted on the Army's proposal. Although JCS promised to re-examine the priorities after RDB conveyed its views on the Hull report, it had in effect granted the Army a substantial part of its original request and all but settled the matter.

The Hull Committee submitted its report to Johnson on 14 September 1949. It contained the stated requirements of the three services and Bradbury's expert opinion that two A-bombs -- a gun and an implosion type -- could be adapted as warheads. The committee emphasized that the armed forces could obtain between two and three times as many implosion as gun-type warheads from the same amount of fissionable materials. on the other hand, implosion warheads were bulkier and heavier and consequently required larger missiles. The committee also believed that four missiles under development--one Army, one Navy, and two Air Force--could be operational about the time warheads became available late in 1953 or early in 1954. Significantly, about that time, fissionable materials would probably be available in quantities sufficient to fill all military demands. Also significant was the finding that the continued development of several missiles were economically and militarily justified only if they carried atomic warheads. The committee recommended close technical liaison between the services and AEC-developing agencies, and also intense studies by DoD on the use and effectiveness of atomic-equipped missiles since little or no information existed on techniques and concepts of employment, types of warheads, fusing, contamination, and the like.[73]

Johnson sent the report to JCS and RDB on 29 September 1949, attaching three questions:

- What missiles should be designated as atomic-warhead carriers?

- What channels of communication and collaboration were needed between DoD and AEC agencies?

- What action should DOD take to evaluate the military worth of the selected missiles? [74]

Joint Staff and RDB representatives studied jointly the several questions but arrived at independent answers. There was little dispute among the services, JCS, and RDB on the broad working and liaison arrangements needed to carry on the cooperative effort with AEC. Agreement also marked the proposal for conducting military worthiness studies of the designated missiles. But a two-week delay in selecting the missiles, while JCS awaited RDB comments on the tentative choices, gave rise to an Army-Air Force misunderstanding that deferred the JCS reply to Johnson for two months. [75]

While awaiting RDB comments, Vandenberg on 22 November 1949 observed that the selection of warheads had been made primarily on the physical dimensions of tentative carriers rather than on the features of the warhead. Noting that gun-type bombs were almost out of production and being removed from stockpiles, he warned that a sizeable requirement for this type of warhead would necessitate expansion of AEC production facilities or reduction of the number of A-bombs in the stockpile. Accordingly, Vandenberg believed that JCS should provide missile development agencies with guidance on warheads, to be determined primarily on the basis of economy of fissionable materials. He suggested that JCS ask the Military Liaison Committee (MLC) to determine the relative desirability of the gun and implosion warheads for specific purposes (air burst, contact, and penetration). [76]

As the Army was planning to use a gun-type warhead, it interpreted Vandenberg's proposal as an attempt to eliminate the Army's missile from the select list. The Army Chief of Staff vigorously asserted that the information Vandenberg wanted from MLC was already available; that JCS, not MLC, should determine what effect the use of the less-efficient gun-type warhead would have on the stockpile and that stockpile considerations alone should not prevent development of all types of warhead. [77]

The Air Staff reply claimed that the Army had misunderstood the intent of Vandenberg's proposal. The Air Force did not oppose selection of the Army's missile as an atomic weapon but only wanted to point out the effects of large gun-type requirements on production goals and the stockpile. JCS should consider this extremely important point, determine the need for gun-types, propose production adjustments, and, if necessary, call for the redesign of missiles to allow incorporation of the most economical warheads. Vandenberg elected not to submit this reply when JGS met on 30 December 1949 to consider action on the Johnson queries. [78]

JCS informed Johnson on this date of its general agreement with the findings of the Hull committee and its urgent call for beginning a coordinated development program. JCS also agreed with the committee's missile selections but thought the weapons should retain the priority ratings assigned them on 25 October. Finally, JCS called for close collaboration and cooperation among AEC, RDB, and the services on the technical problems of the "marriage" and between AEC and the weapons Systems Evaluation Group in evaluating the military effectiveness of the new weapon systems.

Johnson accepted these recommendations and, on 16 January 1950, informed RDB of his desire to place additional emphasis on developing the selected missiles. These were the Navy's Regulus, the Army's Hermes A-3 (a forerunner of Redstone), and the Air Force's Rascal and Snark. In addition, at the suggestion of RDB, Johnson approved a fifth missile – the Army's Corporal E--as an interim weapon to precede Hermes A-3. [79]

Johnson's authorization signaled the beginning of a major effort by the three services to establish atomic warhead requirements for most of their missiles under development. Working closely with a joint group of RDB's committees for guided missiles and atomic energy, the services soon managed to increase greatly the list. They also asked for the development of four, rather than two, warheads -- the originally proposed. gun and implosion types and smaller versions of each. [80]

First atomic artillery shell fired on May 25, 1953 from a specially-designed 280mm howitzer nicknamed "Atomic Annie".

Source: U.S. Army

The favorable OSD and AEC attitude on atomic-equipped missiles encouraged the Army to seek JCS support of what it termed a stop-gap measure until the missiles became operational in 1954 -- the "urgent" development of an atomic artillery shell. The Chief of Naval Operations supported the proposal, except for its urgency. Vandenberg reluctantly agreed even though he considered delivery of atomic bombs by tactical aircraft a far more efficient method of supporting land operations. [81]

In summary, the Air Force had not opposed development of the atomic warhead and shell. Technological advances and the Air Force's own interests dictated against such a step. But Vandenberg and his staff continuously called for caution, emphasizing the need to study carefully the effect of these new demands on the stockpile in terms of use, cost, and effectiveness. Their primary purpose was to insure that in its enthusiastic search for alternate methods to deliver atomic bombs, the Defense Department would retain an adequate inventory to support the nation's primary war deterrent--the strategic air forces.

Planning For Missile Production

Into the swirling arena of study, discussion, compromise, and decision, there entered in 1949 still another aspect of the guided missile program- - production- - or more precisely, mobilization production planning. The Munitions Board, until then inactive in the missile field, first broached the subject after hearing obviously optimistic progress reports from the services. The question of production, facilities, and materials then joined other portions of the missile program as a matter of inter-service dispute.

Early in September 1949, the Munitions Board proposed that a start on planning the allocation of facilities and materials should be made as a first step toward eventual production of guided missiles. The board recognized that the program was still basically experimental, but flight testing would soon require procurement of vehicles in production quantities and many major subsystems and components would remain unchanged in the operational missiles. On this premise, the Munitions Board asked JCS to provide guidance on which the services could formulate mobilization requirements by number and type of missiles. 82

JSPG on 27 September stated that previous JCS guidance for short-range mobilization planning, issued a year earlier to cover a 1949-1950 war, was then being revised. The plan had not listed any missile requirements and neither would the revised plan since only a limited number of World War II missiles could be available for use in 1950. JSPG also reported that long-range plans were under study and it would be some time before JCS acted on them. Finally, RDB was the best source for furnishing a statement on service-test missile requirements. [83]

The Army's member on JSPC opposed these findings, asserting that they failed to provide the Munitions Board and the services with the requisite guidance. He proposed instead that JCS inform the Munitions Board of its intent to make recommendations soon on the long-pending "operational responsibility" question and that these would serve as guidance for the services in computing their requirements. Air Force and Navy committee representatives did not concur, so a split report was sent to JCS on 19 October 1949. [84]

JCS on I November accepted the recommended Navy-Air Force position as the proper one. The next day, it informed the Munitions Board that short-range plans included no missile requirements, long-range plans were still under study, and RDB could provide a statement of test-vehicle requirements. JCS added that until the long-range plans were issued, the Munitions Board, if it wanted, could go directly to the services for approximations of their needs. [85]

The Munitions Board reopened the subject of production planning early in 1950. Encouraged by the results of a joint RDB-Munitions Board review of the missile program, the Munitions Board on 15 February informed Johnson that "extensive production planning is possible at this time and should be pursued aggressively." The board hastened to add that it was thinking in terms of major subsystems and components, not of complete missiles. Johnson asked JCS for comment. [86]

On 24 February 1950, the Munitions Board took a second step by asking JCS to provide the services by I April with a list of required operational missiles, assuming M-Days of I July 1950, 1 July 1952, and 1 July 1953. It also asked the services to compile by 30 April a list of components for the JCS-designated missiles which should go into production at an early date, names of potential contractors, and estimates of cost. The Munitions Board would then consolidate the data and recommend a program of production planning to Johnson by 31 May. [87]

The schedule soon proved unrealistic. JSPG consumed more than a month in deciding on the list of missiles that could be operational by the several M-Days. The group, concerned that list would be used for other than its stated purpose, strongly emphasized that it only provided a basis for selecting components for production planning. Appearance on the list in no way affected existing strategic guidance priorities, and relative importance of any missile. JSPC on 5 April and JCS on 25 April approved the JSPG report and recommendations and sent them to the Munitions Board, RDB, and the three departmental secretaries the next day. [88]

Because JCS did not meet its deadline, the Munitions Board was forced to shift departmental submission dates on several occasions but the departments still failed to meet them. In the case of the Air Force, it was not until 8 July 1950 that Assistant Secretary Stuart finally furnished the required data. The Air Force asserted that missile industrial planning and development progress to date would permit planning for complete missiles rather than only a limited number of selected components. Moreover, influenced by the Korean conflict, the Air Force proposed to conduct production planning studies on all of its missile projects except one. [89]

The Munitions Board spent almost four months digesting and correlating the service plans into a national guided missile mobilization plan. In the interim, the Guided Missiles Interdepartmental Operational Requirements Group had formulated a statement of requirements and sent it to JCS. Realizing that the mobilization plan should complement operational requirements, the Munitions Board on 30 October 1950 sought JCS reaction to its plan in the light of these requirements. Unfortunately, heated disputes among the services over requirements stalled JCS action on the Munitions Board request. [90]

Thus, a premature exercise in missile component production planning begun late in 1949 was overtaken first by the Korean conflict and optimistic missile operational plans and then by inter-service rivalries that hampered development, production, and operational planning. The national mobilization plan lay dormant into 1951 and the likelihood of its adoption then seemed slim as the board's internal missile organization and management realignment set off new inter-service disputes.

VII TRENDS AND RESULTS
By Defense Lion Publications

Looking back over the story that unfolded during this Air Force monograph, it is striking how little resulted from the Air Force campaign to establish a dominant position in the relatively new field of guided missile technology. The long list of programs that were inaugurated at the end of the Second World War was steadily winnowed down until only a handful survived. Of the strategic missiles planned, only Snark and Navaho emerged as anything more than paper studies and neither of these were of any great significance. Navaho was cancelled when the development of ICBMs made it conceptually obsolete. Snark made it into service for barely two months in early 1961 before being declared "obsolete and of marginal military value" by President Kennedy and withdrawn.

Astonishingly, the Air Force air-to-air missile programs were almost as unproductive. Only a single missile, the AIM-4 Falcon, emerged from the Air Force program list and this was only just marginally viable. Originally intended as a bomber defense missile and subsequently adapted to the bomber interceptor role, the AIM-4 suffered severe limitations that circumscribed its operational use. Although deployed in Vietnam aboard F-102 and F-4 aircraft, it proved to be an almost complete failure when used against maneuvering targets. In fairness, it had been designed for use against non-maneuvering targets but the lack of success is still striking. Ironically, the three U.S. air-to-air missiles that dominated the second half of the 20th century, the AIM-7 Sparrow, the AIM-9 Sidewinder and the AIM-120 AMRAAM all had their origins in U.S. Navy projects from the period covered by this book.

The attempted development of surface-to-air missiles was also to prove unproductive. The initial portfolio of Air Force again suffered rapid attrition as funding and political difficulties grew and by the end of the period covered in this book, only one was left. This was the Boeing GAPA and it too was reaching the end of its career. It did, however, give birth to the CIM-10 Bomarc missile that provided strategic air defense for Canada and the United States. Bomarc was a controversial weapon and its actual effectiveness was disputed. It was also the only surface-to-air missile developed by the Air Force and the bulk of American systems in this category came out of U.S. Army programs.

The one really successful Air Force development during the period covered by this book was the MGM-1 Matador tactical support missile. This weapon first flew in January 1949 and was rushed into service as a result of the Korean War. The first operational missiles were delivered in September 1953 to the First Pilot-less Bomber Squadron. More than 1,200 missiles were produced before it was phased out of service in 1962. It was replaced by the MGM-13 Mace that was essentially a Matador with a new and more accurate guidance system.

Why the first generation of Air Force missiles were so unproductive in terms of deployable systems is an interesting question. *The Air Force And The National Guided Missile Program 1944-1950* gives a few clues. One is the pre-occupation of the Army Air Force with its impending establishment as an independent service, co-equal with the Army and Navy. This imposed both technical and political constraints on what could be undertaken with the resources available. Another is that the development programs were conceived under a mind-set that saw guided missile as being pilot-less aircraft. This mind-set was, of course, the underlying reasoning behind the Air Force's desire to dominate the guided missile development field. The Navy and Army attitudes appear to have been quite different; they regarded guided missiles as simply another round of ammunition that happened to be a lot more accurate than earlier ones. In this respect, it is interesting that all the first generation Air Force guided missiles in this book, even the air-to-air systems, look like aircraft. Having got off on the wrong foot, Air Force missile development stumbled.

However, the severity of that stumble should not be overstated. The first generation of missile projects may have been disappointing but they laid the groundwork for a later and much more successful range of weapons. Navaho and Rascal proved the technologies that were later used for the AGM-28 Hound Dog and AGM-69 SRAM missiles. These same technologies later gave birth to the current generation of cruise missiles. These can be seen as a successful implementation of the design concepts first developed in the late 1940s. Today, in the second decade of the 21st century, pilot-less aircraft are a widely-used and deadly part of the American airborne arsenal. Technology has caught up with the visions of those who had conceived the first generation of guided missiles in the 1940s.

There is another striking feature that becomes apparent from this monograph and that is the very limited input from German technology into the Air Force programs. Over the years, a veritable industry has grown up describing the "advanced technology" allegedly developed by the Germans at the end of World War Two. Within this industry it is an article of faith that these alleged German developments "laid the foundation for all existing guided missile technology and ICBM delivery systems." *The Air Force And The National Guided Missile Program 1944-1950* reveals just how false this picture is. Certainly, the operational use of the German V-1 and V-2 missiles did stimulate the post-war surge of interest in guided missiles but in technical terms, it also shows that the U.S. was running at least level with German developments and in some areas had already surpassed them. In actual technology terms, German input to the U.S. Air Force programs was so minimal as to be insignificant. The explosion of missile development in the late 1940s and early 1950s was purely an American achievement.

The following Characteristics Summary and Standard Missile Characteristic sheets cover the three missiles from this period that entered service. It is a historical curiosity that the first, Matador is listed under its bomber designation of B-61 and is described in Standard Aircraft Characteristic format.

Characteristics Summary

BOMBER B-61A

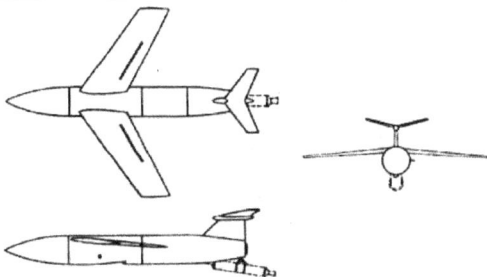

"MATADOR"   MARTIN

Wing Area . . . . 180.0 sq ft   Length . . . . 39.6 ft

Span . . . . 28.7 ft   Height . . . . 9.7 ft

AVAILABILITY			PROCUREMENT			
Number available			Number to be delivered in fiscal years			
ACTIVE	RESERVE	TOTAL				

STATUS

1. Project Initiated: Aug 45
2. First Flight (prod. article): Nov 52
3. First Flight (XSSM-A-1): 19 Jan 49
4. First Flight (YB-61): 22 Dec 50

POWER PLANT

(1) J33-A-37
Allison

THRUST RATINGS
S.L.S.   LB   - RPM - MIN
Max: 4600 - 11,750 - 5
Mil: —   - —   - —
Nor: 4600 - 11,750 - Cont

BOOSTER
No. & Model (1) T-50 Modified
Mfr   Picatinny Arsenal and
Goodyear
Thrust (lb) 57,000
Duration (sec) 2.4

FEATURES

Movable Horizontal Stab-
ilizer
Spoiler Type Ailerons
Honeycomb Wing Construction

Max Fuel Cap: 400 gal

GUIDANCE

SYSTEM
(a) INITIAL:
Programmed air speed
control
(b) MID-COURSE:
MARC (AN/APW-11
used with AN/MSQ-1)
(c) TERMINAL:
Zero lift(ballistic dive)

CONTROL
Electro-hydraulic auto-pilot

The U.S. Air Force & Guided Missiles

Characteristics Summary Basic Mission · · · · · · · · · · B-61A

44,000 FT (Dump point)
35,000 FT
COMBAT FUEL RANGE - 690 N. Mile
See Note (b)

PERFORMANCE

ENDURANCE
1.33 hours

RANGE
690 naut mi.
with 3050 lb payload
at 518 knots avg.
in 1.33 hours

SPEED
MAX 518 knots at 44,000 ft alt, normal power

LAUNCHING
Ground-launched from a zero length launcher with additional boost provided by a T-50 rocket.

PREPARATION & LAUNCH TIME
Approximately 1 1/2 hours

CLIMB
NOT AVAILABLE
fpm sea level, launching wt., max power

NOT AVAILABLE
fpm ft alt, begin cruise wt., max power

ALTITUDE
Begin Cruise 35,000 ft.
End Cruise 44,000 ft.

LOAD
Warhead: 3050 lb

Fuel: 400 gal
protected 0
droppable 0
external 0

WEIGHTS
Empty 5410 lb
Begin Cruise 11,030 lb
End Cruise 8460 lb
Launch 12,660 lb

TARGET ACCURACY
Design criteria requires 95% of the pilotless aircraft launched to arrive in the target area where 50% will strike within 500 ft of target. Present accuracy is approximately 1800 ft.

NOTES

1. PERFORMANCE BASIS:
   (a) Estimated data (Not substantiated by WADC)
   (b) Line-of-sight limitations to microwave propagation restricts the MATADOR with present guidance to 220 nautical miles.

2. REVISION BASIS: To reflect latest characteristics data.

98

Standard Aircraft Characteristics

B-61A

MATADOR

MARTIN

ONE J33-A-37

ALLISON

BY AUTHORITY OF
THE SECRETARY
OF THE AIR FORCE

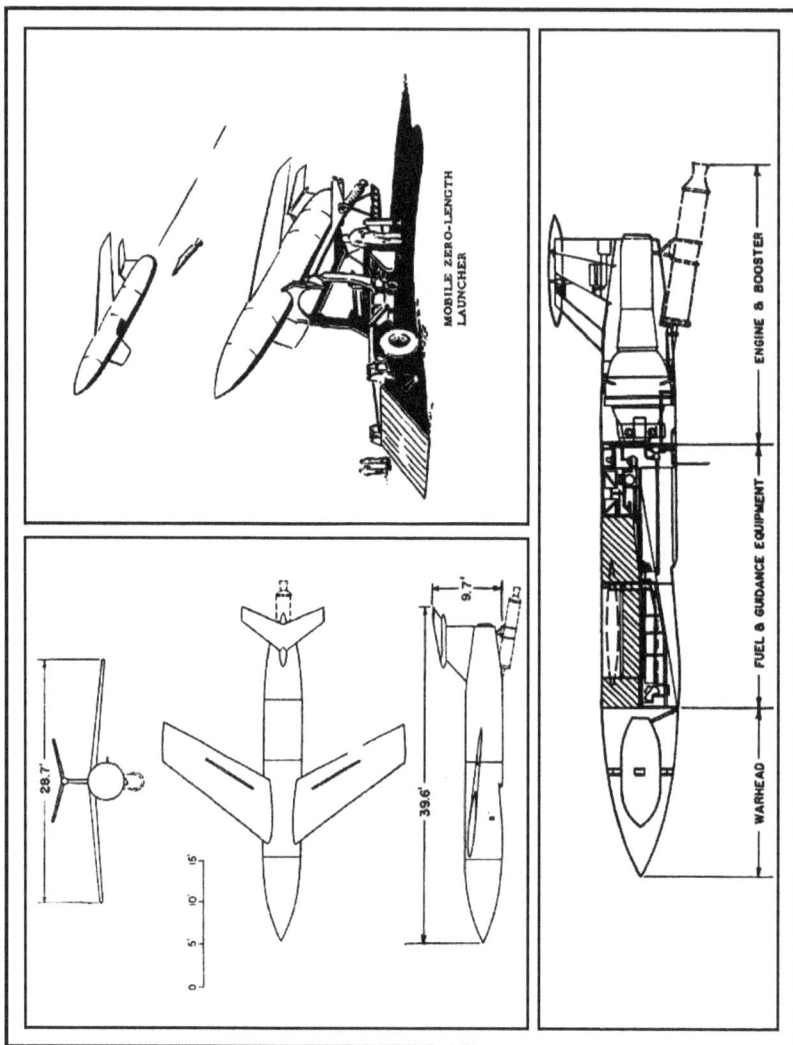

MOBILE ZERO-LENGTH LAUNCHER

28.7'

39.6'

9.7'

ENGINE & BOOSTER

FUEL & GUIDANCE EQUIPMENT

WARHEAD

POWER PLANT

No. & Model		(1) J33-A-37
Mfr.		Allison
Engine Spec No.		318-C
Type		Axial
Length		159.5"
Diameter		49.3"
Weight (dry)		1790 lb

BOOSTER

No. & Model		(1) F-50 modified
Mfr.		Picatinny Arsenal & Goodyear

ENGINE RATINGS

S.L. Static	LB	RPM	MIN
Max	4600	11,750	5
Mil	4600	11,750	Cont
Nor	—	—	—

BOOSTER

S.L. Static	LB	SEC
Max	57,000	2.4

DIMENSIONS

Wing		
Span		28.7'
Length		39.6'
Height		9.7'

Mission and Description

Navy Equivalent: None   Mfr's Model: ——

The MATADOR is a turbo jet powered subsonic pilotless aircraft equipped with a 3000 lb warhead capable of cruising a distance of 690 nautical miles at a cruising speed of at least Mach 0.9 and at a maximum altitude of 44,000 feet.

The basic design is a shoulder wing type airframe with a "T" type tail. Use of honeycomb construction has made it possible to construct thin, smooth contour wing and tail surfaces. Control is maintained by use of a movable horizontal stabilizer and spoiler type ailerons located in the upper surface of the wing.

Presently the MATADOR is limited to operation of 220 nautical miles forward of guidance base stations since guidance depends on line-of-sight microwave transmission. Immediate developmental goal for tactical utility is guidance to within 1000 feet of target. Extension of effective guidance map-matching technique and/or other guidance systems.

Development

Project Initiated	Aug 45
First Flight (XSSM-A-1)	19 Jan 49
First Flight (YB-61)	22 Dec 50
First Flight (B-61A)	Nov 52

Current plans are directed toward operational readiness of two Pilotless Bomber (B-61) Squadrons during FY 1954.

A program has been initiated to include the Shanicle Guidance System in the MATADOR. This configuration uses the B-61C which will replace the B-61A and will contain both Shanicle and MARC. Space, weight and power provisions for Shanicle Guidance is in all B-61A's.

GUIDANCE

SYSTEMS

(a) INITIAL
Programmed air speed control
(b) MID-COURSE
MARC (AN/APW-11 used with AN/MSQ-1)
(c) TERMINAL
Zero lift (ballistic dive)

CONTROL

Electro-Hydraulic Auto-pilot

LAUNCHING

METHOD

Launched to a speed of 200 MPH from a mobile "zero length" launcher. No catapult or runway is required but a RATO booster is used for additional thrust at launch. Pilotless aircraft is supported on the launcher by two forward ball pivots and a cradle at the aft fuselage section.

PREPARATION & LAUNCH TIME

Assembly and check-out by squadron crews will be approximately 20 pilotless aircraft per 8 hour day. Assembled crafts may be stored for 48 hours without rechecks. Ninety minutes will be required for preflight operation.

WEIGHTS

Loading	Lb	L.F.
Empty	5410	
Begin Cruise	11,030	
End Cruise	8460	
Launch	12,660	

BOOSTER

Gross	1630 lb

FUEL

Location	No. Tanks	Gal
Fuselage	3	400
	Total	400

Grade ... 100/130, JP-4 or JP-1
Specification ... MIL-F-5572, MIL-F-5624A or MIL-F-5616

OIL

Fuselage		(tot) 3
Grade		S-1010, W-1005
Specification		MIL-O-6081

WARHEAD

Type	Interchangeable
Weight	3050 lb
Fuze	Barometric

GUIDANCE AND CONTROL

35,000 FT

Mach 0.9

44,000 FT

DUMP POINT

TARGET

LAUNCH
TIME MINUTES   0   100   200   300   400   500   600   690

RANGE — NAUTICAL MILES

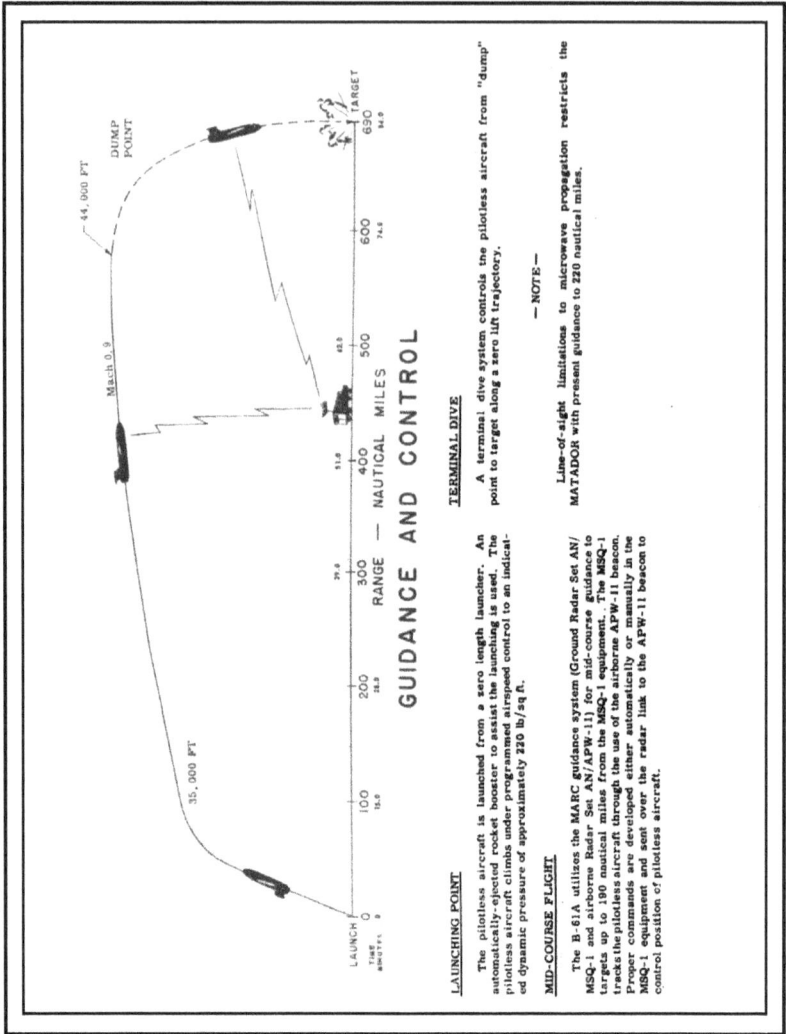

LAUNCHING POINT

The pilotless aircraft is launched from a zero length launcher. An automatically-ejected rocket booster is used to assist the launching. The pilotless aircraft climbs under programmed airspeed control to an indicated dynamic pressure of approximately 220 lb/sq ft.

MID-COURSE FLIGHT

The B-61A utilizes the MARC guidance system (Ground Radar Set AN/MSQ-1 and airborne Radar Set AN/APW-11) for mid-course guidance to targets up to 190 nautical miles from the MSQ-1 equipment. The MSQ-1 tracks the pilotless aircraft through the use of the airborne APW-11 beacon. Proper commands are developed either automatically or manually in the MSQ-1 equipment and sent over the radar link to the APW-11 beacon to control position of pilotless aircraft.

TERMINAL DIVE

A terminal dive system controls the pilotless aircraft from "dump" point to target along a zero lift trajectory.

— NOTE —

Line-of-sight limitations to microwave propagation restricts the MATADOR with present guidance to 220 nautical miles.

Characteristics Summary

STRATEGIC MISSILE SM-62A

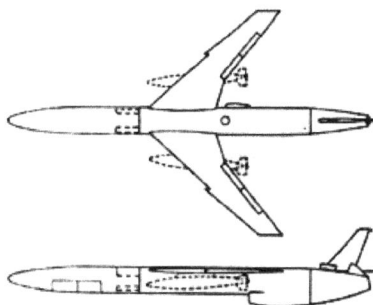

"SNARK"   NORTHROP

Ref Wing Area (does not include leading edge   Length. . . . . 69.9 ft
   or trailing edge extensions) . . 326.0 sq ft
Span . . . . 42.3 ft   Height . . . . 14.8 ft

AVAILABILITY

Number available		
TEST	INVENTORY	TOTAL
3	26	29

PROCUREMENT

Number to be delivered in fiscal years				
FY 61				
6				

STATUS

1. Design Initiated (Guidance System): . Mar 46   6. Last production: . . . . Dec 60
2. First Flight XSM-62: . . . . Aug 53
3. Completion of Cat. I tests: . . . . . Sep 58
4. First prod. delivery to SAC: . . . . Jun 59
5. In prod. - operational: . . . . Mar 60

Navy Equivalent: None   Mfr's Model: N-72

POWER PLANT

(1) J57-P-17
Pratt & Whitney
ENGINE RATINGS
SLS	LB	RPM	MIN
Mil:	10,500	*6150/9900	30**
Norm:	9000	5900/9650	Cont

*Low spool/high spool
**Based on manufacturer's re-
commended limits. For an
engine installed in a tactical
missile, however, no time
limit is imposed since the
engine is considered to be expendable

BOOSTER
Nr & Model. . . . .
. . (2) X-226-A3 Solid Rocket
Mfr. Allegany Ballistics Lab
Thrust . . . . 130,000 lb
Duration . . . . 4 sec

FEATURES

Wing: Low thickness ratio,
high aspect ratio, and high
degree of sweepback. Lateral and longitudinal control
maintained by elevons on
trailing edge.
Fuselage: Houses warhead,
fuel, power plant, and guidance equipment
External Fuel Tanks: Carried
on pylons mounted beneath
the wings and dropped when
empty
Warhead: Delivered through
release of missile ballistic
nose section
Maximum Fuel Capacity: . .
. . . . 3768 gal

GUIDANCE

Model. . . . . . . Mark I*

Mfr . . . .
. . . . Northrop Corp.

Type . . . Inertial, aided by
stellar monitoring
and airmass
damping

*Includes N-80 Autopilot

Characteristics Summary Basic Mission SM-62A

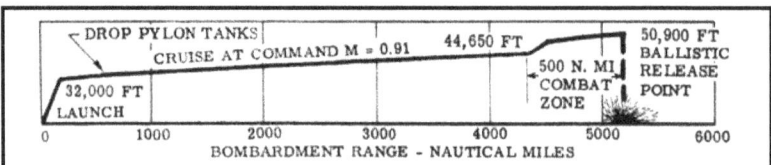

```
 ┌─ DROP PYLON TANKS
 │      CRUISE AT COMMAND M = 0.91    44,650 FT        50,900 FT
                                                       BALLISTIC
                                          500 N. MI.   RELEASE
 32,000 FT                                COMBAT       POINT
 LAUNCH                                   ZONE
 0      1000      2000      3000      4000      5000      6000
          BOMBARDMENT RANGE - NAUTICAL MILES
```

PERFORMANCE

LAUNCHING

Mobile short rail platform
PREPARATION AND LAUNCH
TIME:
Twenty percent of the missile
stockpile will be launched by
D + 1 hour. The balance of the
in-commission missiles will
be launched by D + 3.5 hours.
However during periods of exigency, twenty percent can be
launched in E + 15 minutes, an
additional twenty percent in
E+30 minutes, and the balance
within E + 3 hours. To meet
this requirement, all missiles
will be assembled, launcher-
mounted, fueled, and will have
warheads and boosters installed.

WARHEAD

Type . . . MK-39Y1 Mod-1
Gross Weight . . . . 6230 lb
        FUZE
Type. . Barometric (Air Burst)
    with Impact for backup
Arming Method..Time Heading
                Device

FUEL

Location	No. Tanks	Gal*
Fuselage	8	3038
Ballistic Nose	1	137
Pylon Tanks	2	593
	Total	3768

Grade JP-5
Specification . . . MIL-F-5624C
Usable fuel

RANGE

4910(b)/5322(c) naut mi.

with 6230 lb warhead

at 531/—— knots avg
            cruising speed

in   9.3 hours

CLIMB

3082 fpm at sea level
49,603 lb (launch weight)
military power

1490 fpm at 44,650 ft
25,570 lb (weight at beginning
of high altitude target approach) military power

WEIGHTS

Loading	Lb
Empty(not including warhead)...	16,903
Launch with Pylon Tanks (without boosters)	49,603
Launch with Pylon Tanks (with boosters)...	60,968

SPEED

Climb speed schedule is 365
knots calibrated air speed below 28,400 feet and command
M = 0.91 thereafter. Military
Power is commanded for the
combat zone to give increased
altitude at constant Mach.
number.
540 knots available at military power over the target at
50,900 feet.

ALTITUDE

Launch	Sea Level
Begin Cruise	32,000 ft
End Cruise	44,650 ft
Altitude over the Target	50,900 ft

OPERATIONAL

MAXIMUM OPERA-
TIONAL RANGE

RANGE - NAUTICAL MILES
5400
5300
5200
5100
.5 Probability
Su Fa Wi Sp Su
        Seasons

NOTES

1. Performance Basis:
    (a) Data Source: Flight Test
    (b) ICAO Standard Atmosphere and zero wind.
    (c) Range is the mean value of the operational range.
    (d) Target Accuracy: 50% within 2.0 nautical miles.
2. Revision Basis:
    To reflect latest status information.
3. True Mach number corresponding to 0.91 command Mach number is 0.924.

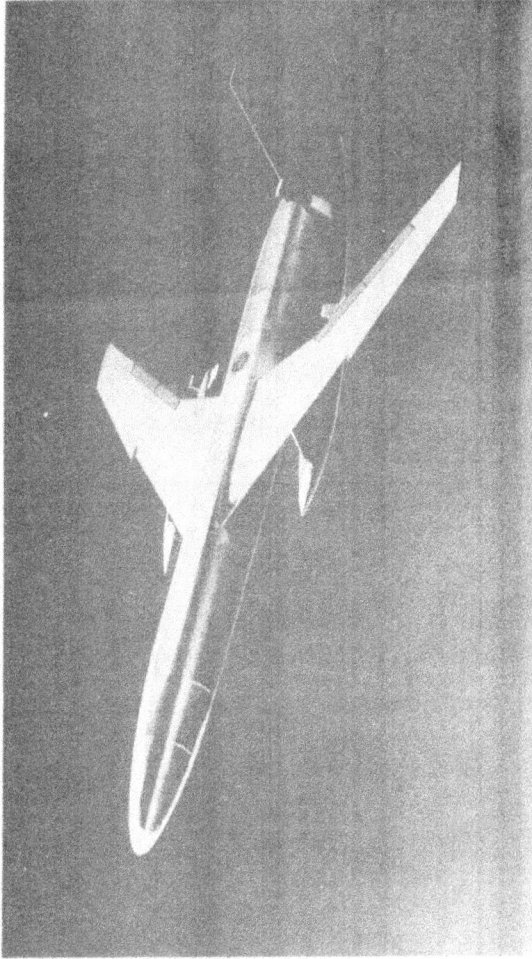

Standard Missile Characteristics

SM-62 A

SNARK
Northrop

J57-P-17

PRATT & WHITNEY

BY AUTHORITY OF
THE SECRETARY
OF THE AIR FORCE

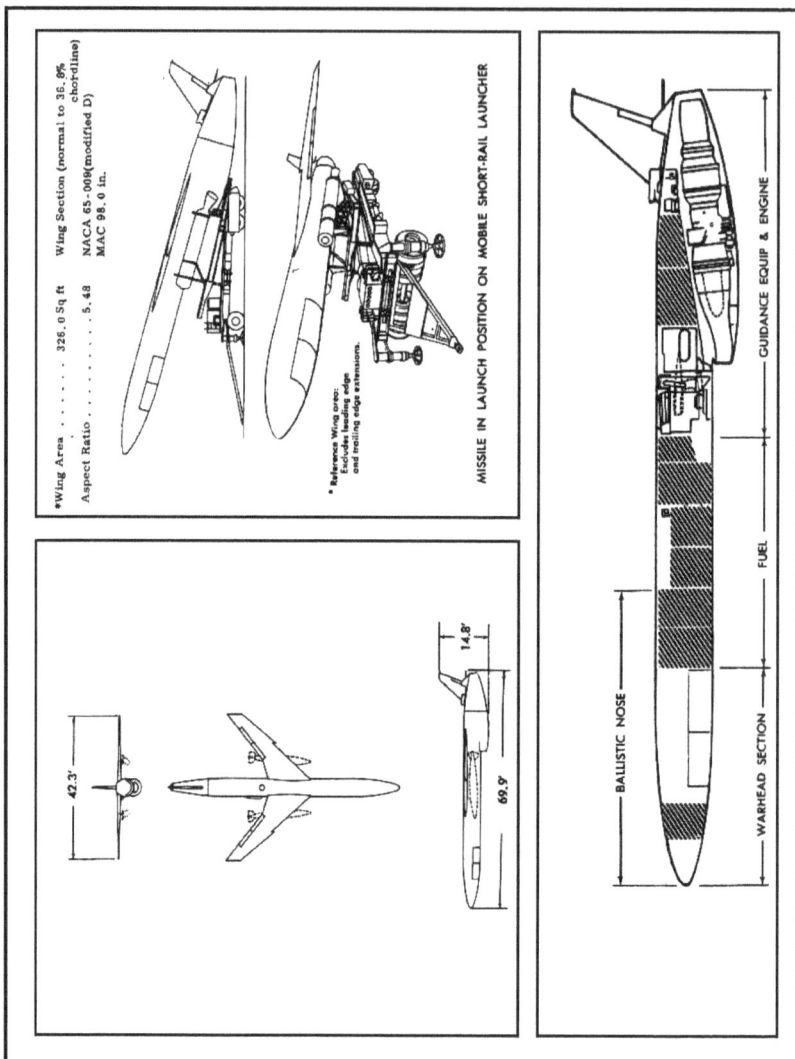

POWER PLANT

Nr & Model .... (1) J57-P-17
Mfr .... Pratt & Whitney
Engine Spec Nr A-1670-D
Type .... Axial Flow
Length .... 161.5 in.
Width .... 40.5 in.
Height .... 48.0 in.
Weight (dry) .... 4175 lb

BOOSTER

Nr & Model ... (2) X-226-A3 Solid Rocket
Mfr .... Allegany Ballistics Lab
Weight (loaded) ...... 5683 lb ea

ENGINE RATINGS

	SL Static Lb	RPM	Min
Mil.	10,500	*6150/9900	**30
Norm.	9,000	9900/9650	Cont

* Low spool/high spool.
** Based on manufacturer's recommended limits. For an engine installed in a tactical missile, however, no time limit is imposed since the engine is considered to be expendable.

BOOSTER

SL Static Lb .... Sec
Max. 130,000 4

DIMENSIONS

Wing
  Span .... 42.3 ft
  Incidence .... 0°
  Dihedral .... 0°
  Sweepback (36.82% chord) .... 45°
Length .... 69.9 ft
Height .... 14.8 ft

Mission and Description

Navy Equivalent: None   Mfr's Model: N-72

The SNARK is a surface-to-surface missile designed to deliver a first-priority warhead on strategic target areas located at distances up to 5500 nautical miles from the launching site, at a speed of 0.91 Mach number and at terminal altitudes of approximately 50,000 feet.

The slender fuselage houses the warhead, fuel, power plant, and guidance equipment. The wing utilizes low thickness ratio, high degree of sweepback, and high aspect ratio. Leading edge extensions of the outboard wing section delay the tip stall. Directional stability is provided by a vertical fin. Longitudinal, lateral and directional control is maintained by means of elevons located on the wing trailing edge. For extended range missions, external fuel tanks are carried on pylons mounted beneath the wings and dropped when empty. The missile is launched from a mobile short rail launching platform by means of booster rockets. The warhead is delivered through release of the missile ballistic nose section during the terminal phase of the flight.

Development

Design Initiated (Guidance System) .... Mar 46
Design Initiated (XSSM-A-3) .... Jan 47
First Flight (XSSM-A-1) .... Jun 50
 .... Mar 51
 .... May 51
 .... Aug 53
Completion of Research & Development .... Sept 58
Availability of Standard Article .... Aug 58

Remarks:
The SM-62A is similar to the later version of the XSSM-A-3A research article (N-69E) except for slight modifications due to production tooling.
The XSSM-A-3A is the XSSM-A-3 experimental article redesigned to incorporate a higher thrust engine and a preproduction airframe configuration.

GUIDANCE

Model .... Mark 1*
Mfr .... Northrop Corporation
Type .... Inertial, aided by
                                  stellar monitoring
                                  and air mass damping
Warhead Delivery .... Ballistic release
                                  of missile nose
                                  section
Terminal Accuracy .... 50% within
                                  2.9 nautical miles

* Includes N-69 Autopilot

LAUNCHING

Mobile short rail platform
Max launch acceleration 3.5 g
PREPARATION AND LAUNCH TIME
Twenty per cent of the missile stockpile will be launched by D-1 hour. The balance of the in-commission missiles will be launched by D+3.5 hours. However, during periods of exigency, 20% can be launched in E-15 min, an additional 20% in E+30 min, and the balance within E-3 hours. To meet this requirement, all missiles will be assembled, launcher-mounted, fueled, and will have warheads and boosters installed.

WEIGHTS

	Lb
Loading	
Empty (not incl warhead)	16,903
Launch with Pylon Tanks (without boosters)	49,603
Launch with Pylon Tanks (with boosters)	66,968

FUEL

Location	Nr Tanks	Gal
Fuselage	8	2038
Ballistic Nose	1	137
Pylon Tanks	2	593
Total		3768

Grade JP-5
Specification MIL-F-5624-C

OIL

	Nr	Gal
Fuselage	2	12

Type .... Synthetic
Specification MIL-C-8188

WARHEAD

Type MK-39Y1 Mod-1
Gross Weight .... 6230 lb

FUZE

Type .... Barometric (Air Burst)
                   with Impact for backup
Arming Method .... Time-Heading
                          Device

Loading and Performance—Typical Mission

		BASIC MISSION (LAUNCH WITH PYLON TANKS) I	EXTENDED COMBAT ZONE MISSION (LAUNCH WITH PYLON TANKS) II	EXTENDED COMBAT ZONE MISSION (LAUNCH WITH PYLON TANKS) III	TYPICAL OPERATIONAL MISSION (LAUNCH WITH PYLON TANKS) IV
LAUNCHING WEIGHT (excluding boosters)	(lb)	49,603	49,603	49,603	49,830
Fuel at 6.5 lb/gal (grade JP-5)	(lb)	25,617	25,617	25,617	25,843
Warhead weight	(lb)	6230	6230	6230	6230
Wing loading (excluding boosters)	(psf)	136.1	136.1	136.1	136.6
Minimum flight speed at SL	(kn)	273.8	273.8	273.8	269.8
Launch altitude	(ft)	SL	SL	SL	SL
Boost thrust and duration	(lb/sec)	260,000/4.0	260,000/4.0	260,000/4.0	260,000/4.0
Rate of climb at SL	(fpm)	3082	3082	3082	3457
Time to climb to 20,000 ft	(min)	8.9	8.9	8.9	7.7
Time to initial cruise altitude	(mm)/(ft)	21.9/32,000	21.9/32,600	21.9/32,000	18.0/31,750
Service ceiling (100 fpm)	(ft)	32,500	32,500	32,500	33,490
BOMBARDMENT RANGE	(n mi)	4910	4790	4590	5280
Average cruising speed	(kn)	531	531	531	561
Final cruising altitude	(ft)	44,630	42,830	39,450	44,730
Total mission time	(hr)	9.30	9.11	8.71	9.26
COMBAT ZONE					
Service ceiling (100 fpm)	(n mi)	500	1000	2000	500
Altitude over target	(ft)	49,050	47,860	44,550	48,890
Speed over target area	(kn)	56,900	56,900	60,900	58,550
Weight over target	(lb)	530	530	530	561
		23,340	23,380	23,380	23,381

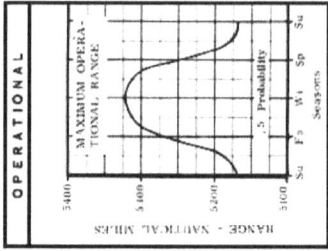

OPERATIONAL — MAXIMUM OPERATIONAL RANGE — .5 Probability — RANGE · NAUTICAL MILES

NOTES

① Military power
② Detailed description of RANGE missions given on page 6
③ Allowance made for weight reduction during launch and climb
④ Limited by maximum usable C_L (0.6)
⑤ Usable fuel
⑥ 0.924 true Mach number
⑦ Military power absolute ceiling
⑧ Operational conditions are:
  a) ANA 432 Polar Atmosphere
  b) fuel density—6.86 lb/gal
  c) Average tailwind—25 knots during cruise and target approach
⑨ Weight at start of military power target approach phase
⑩ Distance for the mean value of the maximum operational range is 5322 nautical miles.

PERFORMANCE BASIS:
a) Data source: Flight Test
b) Performance based on powers shown on page 6
c) Performance is based on ICAO Standard Atmosphere except as noted

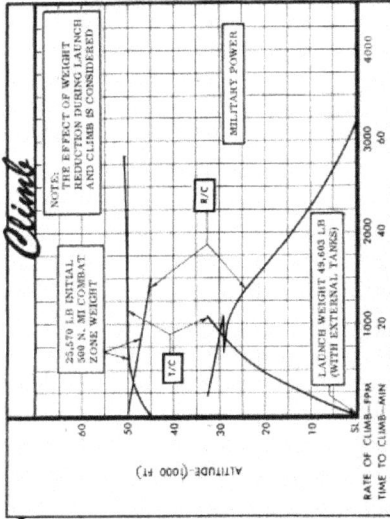

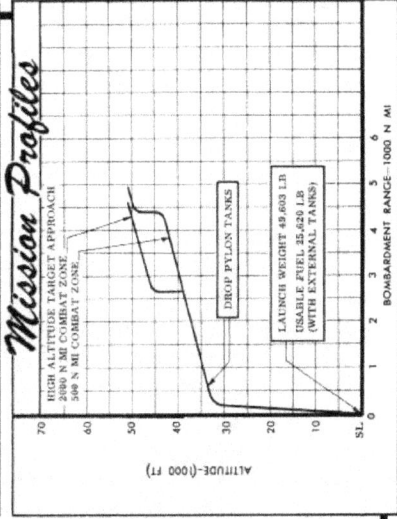

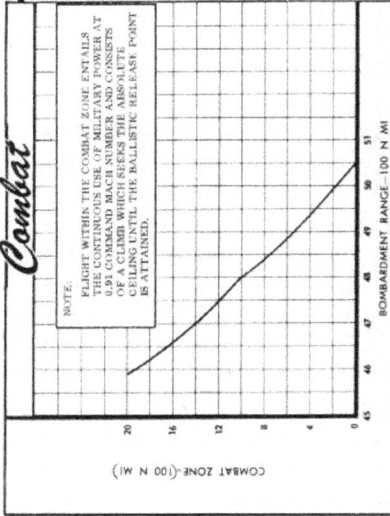

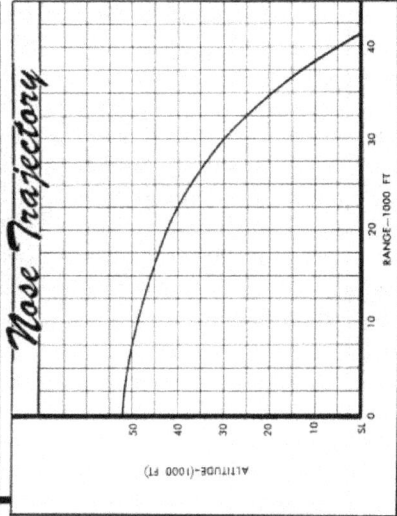

N O T E S

FORMULA: BASIC MISSION I.

Launch, drop boosters, and climb on course to optimum cruise altitude. The climb speed schedule is 365 knots calibrated airspeed below 38,400 ft and 0.81 command Mach number thereafter. Cruise at 0.81 command Mach number until the nose fuel tank and pylon tanks are empty; drop pylon tanks, and continue cruise. The cruise range is determined so that at the conclusion of the 500-nautical-mile combat zone, the missile is at dry weight over the target. Within the combat zone, operation is at military power and 0.91 command Mach number, and consists of a climb toward the absolute ceiling. As the missile nears this ceiling it continues to climb at a slow rate as fuel is used until the 500-nautical-mile distance is attained. The true Mach number corresponding to 0.91 command Mach number is 0.964.

FORMULA: MISSIONS II AND III

Missions II and III are identical to BASIC MISSION I except that the combat zones are 1000 and 2000 nautical miles respectively.

FORMULA: MISSION IV (TYPICAL OPERATIONAL MISSION)

Mission IV is identical to BASIC MISSION I insofar as the mission flight plan is concerned. However, this being an operational mission, specified operational conditions are considered, rather than standard conditions. The missile flight is initiated at the launching site in Maine and extends along the great circle route through Moscow. The mean value of the upper air winds along this route is a 25-knot tailwind. The AKA 633 Polar Atmosphere is considered applicable since it agrees closely with temperatures recorded in the latitude considered for this mission. The additional fuel weight results from the increase in fuel density above the standard value of 6.5 lb/gal to 6.86 lb/gal as determined from NASA samples taken at a storage temperature of 72° F.

GENERAL DATA:

Engine ratings shown on page 3 are the manufacturer's guaranteed sea level static ratings for the J57-P-17 engine. However, performance is based on the following installed ratings:

(1) J57-P-17

SL Static	Lb	RPM(Max)	Min
Mil:	8400	*6150/9900	Cont
Norm:	7300	5900/9650	Cont

*Low spool/high spool

PERFORMANCE REFERENCE:

Northrop Report No. NAI-59-38 "Standard Characteristics and Performance of the SM-62A Strategic Missile," dated 16 December 1959.

REVISION BASIS:

To include additional performance data.

(15 Dec 59)

Guidance and Control

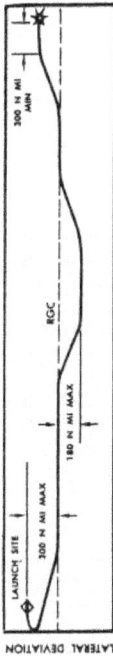

BOMBARDMENT RANGE
TYPICAL FLIGHT PLAN

LATERAL DEVIATION

LAUNCH SITE — 300 N MI MAX — 180 N MI MAX — RGC — 300 N MI MIN

Prior to launch the Reference Great Circle (RGC) is selected on the basis of its proximity to the target area. The missile is launched into the prevailing wind, executes a programmed turn and enters its midcourse climb and cruise. If it is known that certain areas along the flight path are heavily defended, up to three lateral deviations (six heading changes) from the RGC may be programmed in order for the missile to by-pass these defended areas. The initiation of fuel dumping and the high altitude target approach may be combined with the initiation of a lateral deviation in order to obtain maximum utilization of the available range program signals. The missile must be on or parallel to the RGC within 500 nautical miles of the target. The maximum permissible midcourse ground velocity normal to the RGC is 200 knots. At a specified distance from the target, the missile initiates the high altitude target approach. Over the target, the missile executes the pitch-down maneuver required for proper warhead delivery.

FLIGHT PLAN INFORMATION EMPLOYED IN MARK 1 GUIDANCE SYSTEM			
LOCATION	POSITIONAL	METEOROLOGICAL	MAGNETIC
Launch site	Geodetic position and azimuth reference.	None.	None.
Midcourse	Approximate location of defended areas or installations, if it is desired to program evasive deviations from the Reference Great Circle.	Prediction of mean seasonal or monthly railwind over the track at flight altitudes, based on climatological data.	Heading of Reference Great Circle at two selected points, for compass-clock arming system.
Target	Geodetic position and altitude.	Prediction of the height of standard pressure levels, for fuzing.	None.

Characteristics Summary

GUIDED AIRCRAFT ROCKET GAR-4

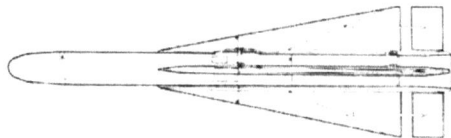

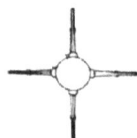

FALCON

HUGHES

Wing Area	Not Applicable	Length	82.5 in
Span	24.0 in.	Height	24.0 in.

AVAILABILITY

Number available

ACTIVE	RESERVE	TOTAL

PROCUREMENT

Number to be delivered in fiscal years

STATUS

1. Extension of GAR- 2 development initiated in March 1954
2. Improved warhead, power supply, and electronic circuitry
3. Improved performance characteristics
4. **In Service: Mid 59**

Navy Equivalent: None

Mfr's Model. GP

POWER PLANT

(1) Two-level Thrust Boost-sustain
Solid Rocket XM18E4

Hughes Aircraft Co.

THRUST RATINGS

S.L.S. @70°F   LB - SEC

Nominal (Average) -

High Thrust Level: 4470-0.61

Low Thrust Level: 670-3.06

High Thrust Level: 4550-0.61

Low Thrust Level;   685-2.95

FEATURES

Passive Infrared Seeker
Faired Sphere Quartz Nirdome

Cruciform Surface Arrangement
"Roll-rate-limiting" Aileron Control

Blast Type Warhead

Contact Fuze

Turbine-driven Electrical and Hydraulic Power Supply

Miniaturized Precision Components and Circuitry

Simplified Fire Control System Capability

Snap-up Capability

Maximum Fuel   **23.3 lb**

GUIDANCE

INITIAL (BOOST PHASE)—
None; Tracking Only

MID COURSE AND TERMINAL—
Homing. Passive Infrared Target Seeker. Proportional Navigation

CONTROL

Hydraulically Actuated Rear Control Surfaces Provide Necessary Steering and Damping
Steering Signals Generated by Target Seeker Tracking Motion

Characteristics Summary Basic Mission GAR-4

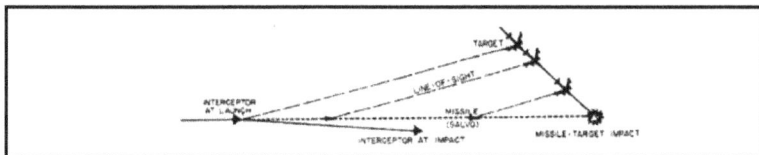

PERFORMANCE

TARGETS	RANGE	SPEED
Subsonic propeller-driven 'or jet bombers Supersonic jet bombers Subsonic or supersonic jet fighters	Nominal missile launch range: 1000 ft to 35,000 ft	MAX Launching aircraft speed plus 1200 fps

LAUNCHING	FLIGHT TIME	ALTITUDE
Short-length tracks (4) extended from F-106A fuselage bay 16 sec minimum preparation time from AI radar detection Salvos of 2 missiles	Nominal missile flight time: 3.5 sec to 22.0 sec	Effective up to 70,000 ft

LOAD	WEIGHTS	TARGET ACCURACY
Warhead and Fuze (installed).... 10.3 lb Explosive.............5.00 lb Motor (loaded)........39.4 lb Useful Fuel..........23.3 lb	Empty.............. 94.8 lb Pre-launch.......... 132.0 lb End of Boost Phase....119.3 lb Burnout............ 108.4 lb	P_k — 0.87 for salvo of 2 missiles in rear hemisphere attacks against subsonic and supersonic bombers

NOTES

1. Performance Basis:
    (a) Calculation based on experimental FALCON flight tests, component tests, and estimated data.
    (b) NACA standard atmospheric conditions.

2. Revision Basis: To change characteristics data.

3. Probability of kill (P_k) value is based upon 90% missile reliability and 0.90 kills per hit.

4. Nominal values correspond to idealized operation of the fire control system.

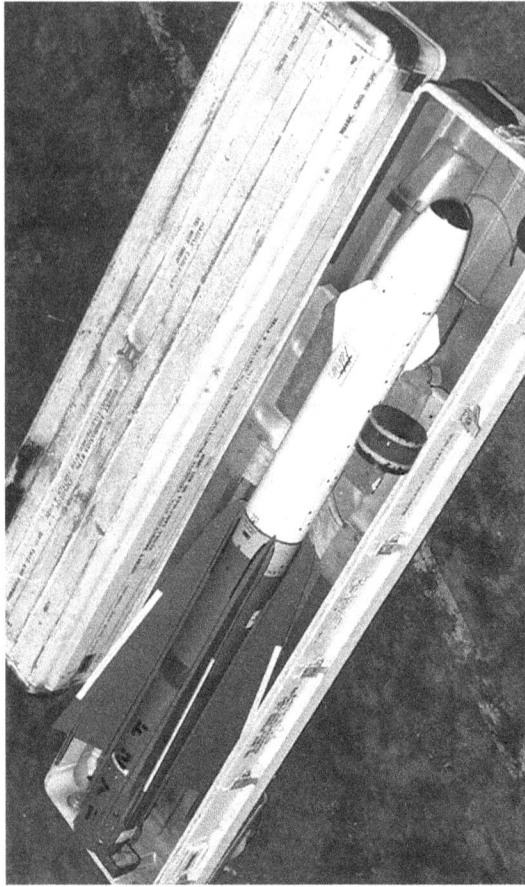

Standard Missile Characteristics

GAR-4
FALCON
HUGHES

ONE SOLID ROCKET XM18E4
HUGHES

BY AUTHORITY OF
THE SECRETARY
OF THE AIR FORCE

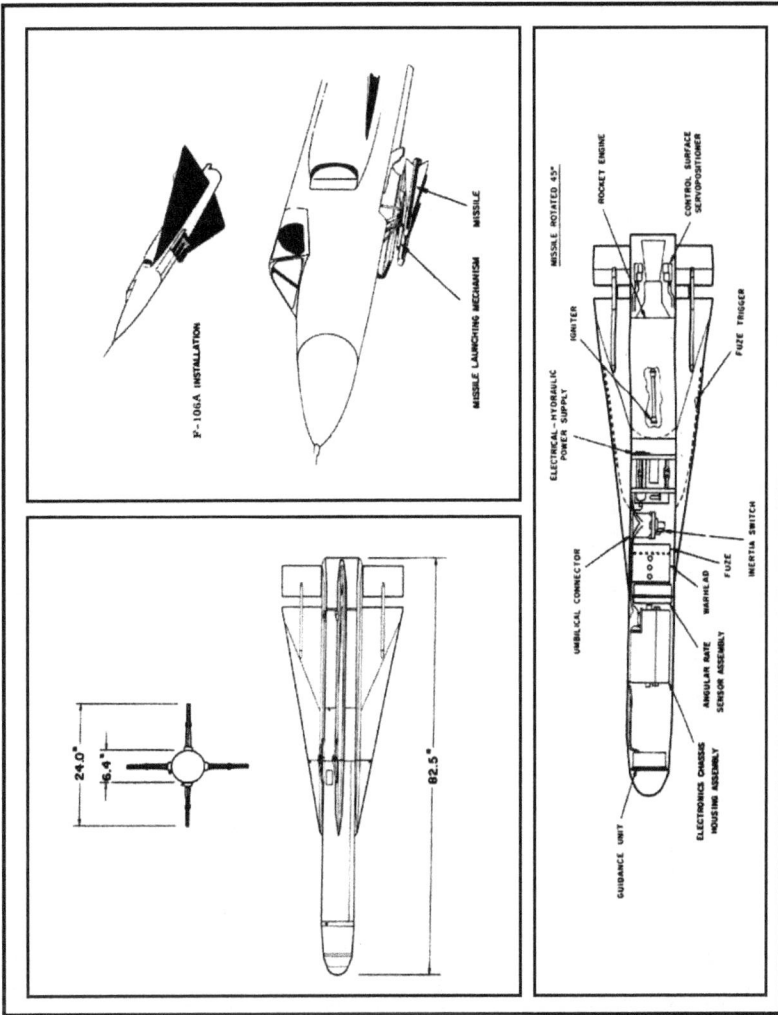

F-106A INSTALLATION

MISSILE LAUNCHING MECHANISM

MISSILE

MISSILE ROTATED 45°

ROCKET ENGINE

CONTROL SURFACE
SERVOPOSITIONER

IGNITER

FUZE TRIGGER

ELECTRICAL—HYDRAULIC
POWER SUPPLY

INERTIA SWITCH

FUZE

UMBILICAL CONNECTOR

WARHEAD

ANGULAR RATE
SENSOR ASSEMBLY

ELECTRONICS CHASSIS
HOUSING ASSEMBLY

GUIDANCE UNIT

24.0"

6.4"

82.5"

POWER PLANT

Nr & Model	(1) Solid Rocket XM-18E4
Mfr.	Hughes Aircraft Co.
Engine Spec Nr	SRSM9-195
Type	Two-level Thrust Boost-sustain
Length	28.45 in.
Diameter	6.400 in.
Weight (loaded)	39.4 lb
Flight Operating Conditions	
Temperature	40 to 160°F
Altitude	S.L. to 70,000 ft

ENGINE RATINGS

S.L. Static @ 70°F	LB	SEC
Nominal (Average)—		
High-thrust Level:	4550	0.61
Low-thrust Level:	685	2.95
Impulse (lb-sec)—		
High-thrust Level		2795
Low-thrust Level		2015
Total		4815
Over all Specific Impulse (lb-sec/lb)		122

DIMENSIONS

Span	24.0 in.
Length	82.5 in.
Height	24.0 in.
Diameter	6.4 in.

Mission and Description

Navy Equivalent None   Mfr's Model: GPa

The GAR-4 (FALCON) is a small supersonic guided aircraft rocket whose prime mission is the destruction of subsonic and supersonic bombers.

It is air-launched from F-106A interceptors.

The GAR-4 is similar to the GAR-3 except that a passive infrared target seeker system is installed in lieu of a semi-active radar system. An infrared telescope is mounted on the seeker gyroscope in place of the radar antenna. A quartz airdome replaces the plastic radome. The electronic frequency converter unit is removed and several chassis in the electronics package replaced in order to effect integration of the infrared seeker system with the remainder of the control system. All other components of the GAR-4 are the same as those used in the GAR-3.

Development

The salvo of 2 rockets is launched forward from the interceptor on a lead-collision course depends upon a direct hit for detonation. The GAR-4 has an optimized launching range of 1000 ft to 35,000 ft, dependant on altitude, maximum speeds at end of rocket burning, and fire control system. The tactical weapon is effective at altitudes up to 70,000 feet.

The GAR-4 is an extension of the GAR-2 development and was initiated in March 1954. Changes include an improved warhead, a miniature turbine unit to provide electric and hydraulic power, and many electronic improvements. Development of this particular rocket will parallel that of the GAR-3.

GUIDANCE AND CONTROL

Type—		
Initial (Boost Phase)	None	
	Tracking Only	
Mid course and Terminal	Homing	
	Passive Infrared	
Target Seeker	Proportional Navigation	
Wavelength	1.8 to 2.7 Microns	
Electrical Power Source	Turbine Generator	
Type	4 Rear Control Surfaces	
Method	4 Hydraulic Servopotentiometers	
Hydraulic Power Source	Turbine Pump	
Horizontal Surfaces	Steering and Damping in Pitch	
	Passive Infrared	Steering and Damping in Yaw
Vertical Surfaces	Steering and Damping in Roll	
	Damping in Roll	

LAUNCHING

Method	Short-length Track, Launching Hooks on Missile Body
Launcher Location	Fuselage Bay
Maximum Launching Preparation Time from AI Radar Detection	16 sec

WEIGHTS

	LB
Loading	
Empty	94.8 (E)
Pre launch	132.9 (E)
End of Burst Phase	119.3 (E)
Burnout	108.4*(E)
(E) Estimated	
* Includes 0.3 lb Liner Burned	

FUEL

Useful Weight (lb)	21.3
Type	Thiokol TRX-139G
Specification	Thiokol SP-88
Specific Impulse (lb-sec/lb)	205*
*S.L. @ 70° F	

WARHEAD

Type	Blast
Installed Weight (lb)	19.3*
Explosive—	
Type	HBX-3
Weight (lb)	5.00
*Including Fuze and Arming Pistol	
Type	Contact
FUZE	
Target Location	Stabilizer LE
PROBABILITY OF KILL	
Average (Rear Hemisphere Attacks)	0.87 for Salvo of 2 Missiles

Loading and Performance—Typical Mission

Launch Airplane		F-106A ⑥		Supersonic Bomber ④	
Target Type		Subsonic Jet Bomber		Supersonic Bomber	
Missile Weights:					
Pre-launch	(lb)	132		132	
End of Boost Phase	(lb)	119.3		119.3	
Burnout	(lb)	108.4		108.4	
Warhead and Fuze	(lb)	10.3		10.3	
Launch Airplane Weights:					
Guidance System ⑤	(lb)	2017		2017	
Missile Auxiliaries	(lb)	145		145	
Launchers (4)	(lb)	102		102	
Altitude	(ft)	30,000	45,000	30,000	55,000
Target Mach Number		0.90	0.81	1.67	1.46
Maximum Target Load Factor	(g's)	NA ①	NA	NA	NA
Missile Mach Numbers:					
Launch		1.85	1.96	1.85	1.63
Maximum		2.83	3.14	2.82	2.96
Maximum Missile Load Factor	(g's)	24.6	24.2	24.6	18.0
Aspect Angle	(deg)	180 (tail)	180 (tail)	180 (tail)	180 (tail)
Nominal Missile Terminal Mach Number		1.94	2.28	2.71	2.38
Missile Load Factor at Nominal Terminal Mach Number ⑦	(g's)	16.5	15.9	23.7	14.0
Ranges:					
Minimum Missile Air Range	(ft)	2,200	2,100	3,100	2,800
Maximum Missile Air Range	(ft)	42,600	47,300	30,000	44,300
Minimum Missile Launch Range	(ft)	1,050	1,090	1,000	1,450
Maximum Missile Launch Range	(ft)	24,000	31,500	19,660	18,900
Nominal Missile Launch Range	(ft)	20,870	22,850	5,090	16,750
Flight Times:					
Minimum Missile Flight Time	(sec)	1.3	1.3	1.3	1.3
Maximum Missile Flight Time	(sec)	20.0	20.0	11.3	20.0
Nominal Missile Flight Time	(sec)	12.8	11.0	5.5	16.0
Probability of Hit ② per Missile for Target Maneuver of 32 ft/sec²	③	0.80	0.80	0.80	0.80
Probability of Kill per Missile for Target Maneuver of 32 ft/sec²	③	0.64	0.64	0.64	0.64

① NA—not available.
② Based upon 100% missile reliability.
③ Preliminary estimates.
④ Hypothetical supersonic bomber having maximum speeds equal to 90% of the corresponding F-106A maximum speeds.
⑤ MA-1 Fire Control System.
⑥ Composite characteristics of B-47 and B-52 jet bombers.
⑦ 45° Roll Angle
⑧ Detailed description of typical mission, target radiation characteristics used, and general notes are given on page 6.

PERFORMANCE BASIS:
Ⓐ Data Source: Calculation based on experimental FALCON flight tests, component tests, and estimated data.

NOTES

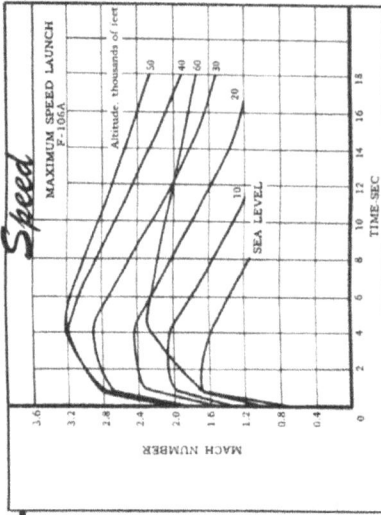

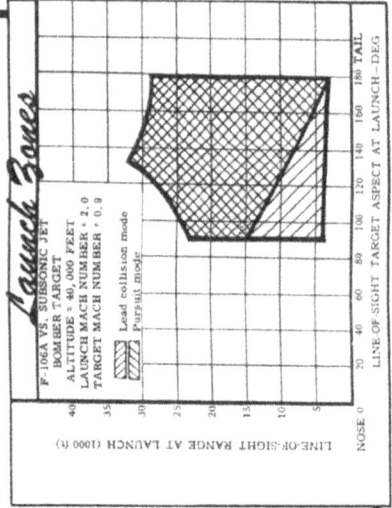

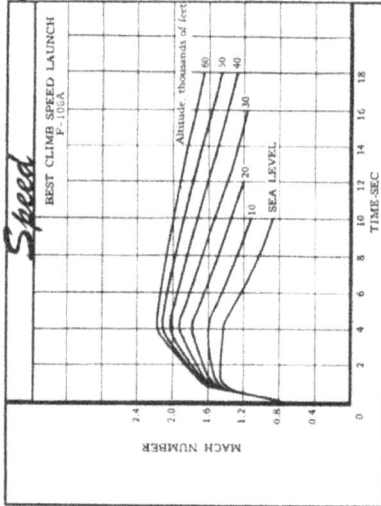

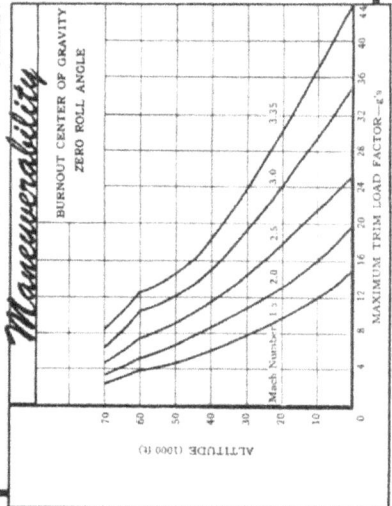

NOTES

CHAPTER 1

1. Material for this chapter came primarily from two sources: *The Development of Guided Missiles*, prepared by Mary R. Self and published by the AMC Historical Division, 1946, and Chapter VII *Men and Planes, Volume VI, the Army Air Forces in World War Two* (Univ. of Chicago Press, 1955).

CHAPTER 2

1. Ltr, CG, AGF to CG, ASF, 9 Feb 44, subj: Development of Anti-aircraft Materiel; memo, Ch/Ord to CG, ASF, 26 May 44, subj: Long-Range Rocket and Launching Equipment -- Initial Development Project, Recommended; ltr, Lt Col R.A. Meredith, Asst AG, AGF to CG, ASF, 22 Jul 44, subj: Development of Guided Missiles for Artillery Employment; memo for record by Col E. B. Gallant, OPD, WDGS, 23 Sep 44, subj: Guided Missiles; memo, Brig Gen W.A. Borden, Dir, NDD, WDSS to DCIS, USAF, 26 Sep 44, subj: Guided Missiles.

2. Memo, R.A. Lovett, Asst Secy/War for Air to Gen H.H. Arnold, CG, AAF, 2 Aug 44, subj: Pilot-less Aircraft and Guided Missiles; informal note, Arnold to Maj Gen H.A. Craig, AC/AS, O, C&R, about 3 Aug 44, no subj; memo E. L. Bowles, Expert Consultant to Secy/War to Col S.F. Giffin, Exec, Reqs Div, AC/AS, O,C&R, 7 Aug 44, no subj; draft memo for Asst Secy/War for Air Prep by Col S.F. Giffin, 11 Aug 44, subj: Pilot-less Aircraft and Guided Missiles; memo, Craig to C/AS 14 Aug 44, subj: Pilot-less Aircraft and Guided Missiles"

3. Memo, Gen H.H, Arnold, CG, AAF to R.A. Lovett, Asst Secy/War for Air, 17 Aug 44, subj: Pilot-less Aircraft and Guided Missiles.

4. R&R, Brig Gen Donald Wilson, Actg C/AS to AC/AS, M&S, 17 Aug 44, subj: Development of Self-Propelled Guided Missiles.

5. Ltr, Col R. C. Wilson, Ch, Dev Eng Br, AC/AS, M&S to CG, MC 2 Aug 44, subj: Combining AAF and Ordnance Experience on Guided Missiles; ltr, CG, MC to CG, AAF, 22 Aug 44, subj: Combining AAF and Ordnance Experience on Guided Missiles.

6. R&R-2, Maj Gen O. P. Echols, AC/AS, M&S to C/AS, 25 Aug 44, subj: Development of Self-Propelled Guided Missiles; memo, Col J.F. Phillips, Ch, Mat Div, AC/AS, M&S to Brig Gen E.M. Powers, Dep AC/AS, M&S, 5 Sep 44, subj: Proposed Memorandum for the Chief of Staff on Guided Missiles; draft memo, AC/AS, M&S to AC/AS, O, C&R, 5 Sep 44, subj: Proposed Memorandum for the Chief of Staff on Guided Missiles.

7. Memo, Lt Gen B. M. Giles, C/AS to U/Secy/War, 7 Sep 44, subj: Development of Self-Propelled Guided Missiles; memo, Giles to Ch/ Ord, 7 Sep 44, subj: Development of Self-Propelled Guided Missiles.

8. Summary Sheet, Brig Gen M.A. Borden, Dir, NDD, WDSS to G-I, G-2, G-3, WDGS, 14 Sep 44, subj: Guided Missiles; memo for record by Gallant, 23 Sep 44; memo, Borden to DC/S, USA, 26 Sep 44.

9. Memo, Borden to DG/S, USA, 26 Sep 44.

10. Memo, Lt Gen J.T. McNarney DC/S, USA to CG's, AAF, AGF, and ASF, 2 Oct 44, subj: Guided Missiles.

11 Memo, Brig Gen W.A. Borden, Dir, NDD, WDSS to Lt Gen T. T. Handy, DC/S, USA, 17 Jan 45, subj: Guided Missiles; memo, Col H.I. Hodes, Asst DC/S, USA to Dir, NDD, 19 Jan 45, subj: Guided Missiles.

12. ASSS by Col S.F. Giffin, Reqs Div, ACIAS, O,C&R, 5 Feb 45, subj: Major Command Responsibility for Employment of Guided Missiles; draft DF by Giffin, 23 Jan 45, subj: Guided Missiles; memo, Brig Gen F.H. Smith, DC/AS to Brig Gen R.C. Hood, DC/AS, 25 Jan 45, no subj; DF, Lt Gen B.M, Giles, Dep Comdr, AAF to OPD, WDGS, 28 Jan 45, subj: Guided Missiles.

13. Memo, Col J.C. Daly, Actg Ch, Log Gp, OPD to CG, AAF, 30 Jan 45, subj: Guided Missiles; memo for record by Daly, 31 Jan. 45, subj: Guided Missiles; memo, Daly to AC/S, G-3, 31 Jan 45, subj: Guided Missiles.

14. Memo, Col W. F. McKee, Actg AC/AS, O, C&R to Brig Gen R. C. Hood, DC/AS, 3 Feb 45, no subj; ASSS by Giffin, 5 Feb 45; DF (and attached draft memo), Lt Gen B. M. Giles, C/AS to G-3, WDGS, 6 Feb 45, subj: Guided Missiles.

15. DF, Maj Gen I. H. Edwards, AC/S, G-3 to CG, AAF, 19 Mar 45, subj: Guided Missiles; memo, Edwards to CG's, AAF, AGF, and ASF, 19 Mar 45, subj: Guided Missiles.

16. Memo, Edwards to CG's, AAF, AGF, and ASF, 19 Mat 45.

17. Memo, Brig Gen P.W. Timberlake, DC/AS to C/S, USA, 24 Mar 45, subj: Guided Missiles; memo, Maj Gen Donald Wilson, AC/AS, O, C&R to C/AS, 26 May 45, subj: Responsibility for Operational Employment of Guided Missiles; memo, Brig Gen R. C. Hood, DC/AS to C/AS, 28 May 45, no subj; memo, Lt Gen I.C. Eaker, Dep Comdr, AAF to C/S USA, 1 Jun 45, subj: Responsibility for Operational Employment of Guided Missiles.

18. Memo, Maj Gen I.H. Edwards, AC/S, G-3 to DC/S, USA, I Jun 45 subj: operational Employment of Guided Missiles (with an attached draft memo for dissemination to the three Army forces); memo, Brig Gen H.I. Hodes, Asst DC/S, USA to AC/S, G-3, ZI Jun 45 subj: Responsibility for the Operational Employment of Guided Missiles.

19. Memo, Lt Col G.W. Hill, Exec, AC/AS, O, C&R to Dep ACIAS O, C&R, 30 Jun 45, subj: Operational Employment of Guided Missiles (with attached draft Arnold to Marshall memo).

20. Memo, Brig Gen W.F. McKee, Dep AC/AS, O, C&R to Lt Gen H.S. Vandenberg, ACIAS, O, C&R, 3 Jul 45, no subj; memo, Maj. W.W. Proust, office of AC/AS, O, C&R, to Col Sweetser, office of AC/AS, O, C&R, 9 Jul 45, no subj.

21. R&R, Brig Gen A.R. Crawford, Ch, Prod Div, AC IAS-4 to Office of GM's, AC/AS-4, 27 Aug 45, subj: Division of Army Responsibility on Guided Missiles Research and Development; memo, Crawford to Maj Gen E.M. Powers, AC/AS-4, 24 Sep 45, subj: Necessity for an Army Air Forces Air Defense Policy; R&R, Crawford to AC/AS-3, 1 Oct 45, subj: Recommended Assignment of Guided Missiles Development Responsibility in the Army (with attached draft memo for C/S, USA, 1 Oct 45 (an expanded version was dated 8 Oct 1945); memo, V.S. Roddy, GM Br, AC/AS-4 to GM Br, AC/AS-4, 2 Nov 45, no subj; memo, Crawford to C/AS, 4 Dec 45, subj: Preparation of A.A.F. Policy on Guided Missiles.

22. Memo, Maj Gen Lauris Norstad, AC/AS-5 to C/AS, 26 Nov 45, subj: Functions and Responsibilities of the U.S. Army Air Forces.

23. R&R, Crawford to AC/AS-3, 1 Oct 45; memo, Crawford to C/AS 4 Dec 45; R&R, Maj Gen Lauris Norstad, Ac/As-5to AC/AS-4, 19 Dec 45, subj: Proposed Memo for the Chief of Air staff on Preparation of AAF Policy on Guided Missiles Development, Operations, and Countermeasures.

24. Memo, Col T.A. Sims, Exec, C/AS to DC/AS 2 Jan 46, subj: Guided Missiles; Minutes of (Air) Staff Meeting, 3 Jan 46.

25. Memo, Col M.F. Cooper, Ch, GM Br to Ch, Res & Eng Div, AC/AS, about 28 Jan 46, no subj.

26. Memo, Brig Gen H.I. Hodes, Asst DC/S to CG's, AAF, AGF, and ASF, 13 Feb 46, subj: Policy on Research and Development of Guided Missiles.

27. Memo, Gen Carl Spaatz, CG, AAF' to DC/S, USA, 4 Mar 46, subj: Policy on Research and Development of Guided Missiles.

28. Memo, CG, AGF to C/S, USA, 27 Eeb 45, subj: Policy on Research and Development of Guided Missiles; memo, Brig Gen A.R. Crawford, Ch, Res & Eng Div, AC/AS-4 to DC/AS for R&D, 26 Mar 46, subj: Policy on Research and Development of Guided Missiles.

29. Memo, Crawford to DG/AS for R&D, 26 Mar 46.

30. R&R, Lt Gen I. C. Eaker, Dep Comdr, AAF to all AC/AS, 2 Apr 46, subj: Policy on Research and Development of Guided Missiles; memo, Gen Carl Spaatz, CG, AAF to C/S, USA, 29 Apr 46, subj: Policy on Research and Development of Guided Missiles (with attached draft memo to CG's, AAF, AGF, and ASF); memo, Spaatz to Maj Gen Donald Wilson, CG, AAFPGC, 29 May 46, no subj; WD Circ 138, 14 May 46; R&R, Maj Gen C.E. LeMay, DC/AS for R&D to Res & Eng Div, 12 Jun 46, subj: Briefing in War Dept. Duplication of Effort on Research and Development Projects; rpt, Prepared Briefing for General Aurand, 12 Jul 46, prep by Brig Gen A.R. Crawford, Ch,

Res & Eng Div, AC/AS-4; informal memo, Col M.F. Cooper, Ch, GM Br to Crawford, about 20 Jul 46, no subj.

31. Memo, Maj Gen C. E. LeMay, DC/AS for R&D, AAF to Ch/Ord, USA, et al, 14 Aug 46, subj: Coordination of Guided Missiles Development; memo for record by Brig Gen 'W'L.. Richardson, Ch, GM-Air Def Div, AS/AC-3, 5 Sep 46, subj: Duplication in Guided Missiles Research and Development.

32. Memo, Maj Gen C.E. LeMay, DC/AS for R&D to CG, AAF, 20 Sep 46, subj: Guided Missiles.

33. New York Times, 10 Aug 46; msg, WAR 82213, Lt Gen T. T. Handy, DC/S, USA to Gen D.D. Eisenhower, C/S, USA, 3 Oct 46, no subj; Washington Post, 9 Oct 46; New York Times, 9 Oct 46.

34. Msg, WAR 82213, 3 Oct 46.

35. Memo, Maj Gen C.E. LeMay, DG/AS for R&D, AAF to Dir/R&D, WDGS, 30 Sep 46, subj: Development of Guided Missiles (with attached draft memo).

36. Msgr WAR 82213, 3 Oct 46; memo, Brig Gen H.I. Hodes, Asst DC/S, USA to CG's, AAF and AGF, and Chiefs, all Tech Svcs, 7 Oct 46, subj: Guided Missiles.

37. Washington Post, 9 Oct 46; New York Times, 9 Oct 46.

38. Memo, Maj Gen H.S. Aurand, Dir/R&D, WDGS to CG, AAF, Ch/ Ord, & Ch Sig Officer, 10 Oct 46, subj: Review of Guided Missiles Projects; memo, Aurand to CG's, AAF and AGF, and Chiefs, all Tech Svcs, 26 Nov 46, subj: Guided Missiles -- Responsibilities and Procedures.

39. Memo, Aurand to GG, AAF at al, 26 Nov 46.

40. Memo, Maj Gen C.E. LeMay DC/AS for R&D to Exec, Asst Secy/War for Air, 17 Jun 47, subj: Guided Missile Program; ltr, Maj Gen B. W. Chidlaw, Chmn, AAFTC to CG, AAF, 18 Jul 47, subj: War Department Guided Missile Research and Development.

41. Memo, CG, AGF to G/S, 26 Aug 46, subj: Operational Employment of Ground Launched Guided and Homing Missiles; memo, CG, AGF to C/S, 15 Oct 46, subj: Responsibility for Establishing Military Characteristics for Ground-Launched Guided Missiles; memo for record by Col E.J. Rogers, Ch, Policy Div, AC/AS-5, 7 Oct 46, subj: Policy on Guided Missiles; memo Brig Gen W. L. Richardson, Ch, GM Div, AC/AS-3 to AG/AS-3. 18 Nov 46, subj: Guided Missiles Material for Presentation at Commanders Meeting; AGF study Operational Employment of Ground-Launched Guided Missiles, 13 Jan 47.

42. USAF Hist Study 126, The Development of Continental Air Defense to September 1954, by C. L. Grant, USAF Hist Dic, pp 15 - 16

43. Ibid.; WD Circ 138, 14 May 46.

44. Rpt, Security from Enemy Air Action, by AGF, 14 Jun 46; Ltr, Gen Carl Spaatz, CG, AAF to CG, AGF, 11 Jul 46, subj: Responsibility for Air Defense (with attached comments-on AGF rpt of 14 Jun); DF, Gen J. L. Devers, CG, AGF to CG, AAF, 9 Aug 46, subj: Responsibilities for Air Defense.

45. WD Staff Summary, Dir/O&T Div to C/S, USA, 18 Sep 46, subj: Responsibilities for Air Defense; DF, C/S, USA to CG, AAF, 24 Sep 46, subj: Responsibilities for Air Defense; USAF Hist Study 126, p 17.

46. Ltr, Gen Carl Spaatz, CG, AAF to CG, AGF, 9 Oct 46, no subj.

47. Ltr, Gen J. L. Devers, CG, AGF to CG, AAF, 14 Oct 46, no subj.

48. Ltr, Gen Carl Spaatz, CG, AAF to CG, AGtr',24 Oct 46, no subj.

49. Ltr, Brig Gen A.R. Crawford., Ch, MatDiv, AC/AS, M&S to CG, ATSC, 23 Aug 45, subj: Countermeasures Against Guided Missiles; memo, Crawford to Maj Gen E. M. Powers, AC /AS-4, 24 Sep 45, subj: Necessity for an Army Air Forces Air Defense program.

50. Memo, Gen H.H. Arnold, CG/AAF to AC/AS-3 and DC/AS for R&D, about 21 Nov 45, no subj.

51. Ltr, Gen D.D. Eisenhower, C/S, USA to CNO, 13 Feb 46, no subj; ltr, Adm C.W. Nimitz, CNO to C/S, USA, 27 Feb 46, no subj.

52. Memo, Lt Gen Lauris Norstad, AC/AS-5 to CG, AAF, about 15 Feb 46, no subj; memo, Spaatz to DC/S, USA, 4 Mar 46.

53. Rpt, Review of Responsibilities for Research and Development, prep by Navy, 18 Mar 46.

54. GMC Rpt 17 /3, 23 Apr 46; memo, Bradley Dewey, Chmn, GMC to GMC, 13 Apr 46, subj: Allocation of Research and Development Responsibility; ltr, Adm C.W. Nimitz, CNO to C/S, USA, L4 Jur.46, no subj.

55. Precept, Aero Bd,, 22 Aug 45; memo, Secy, Aero Bd to Members, subcmte of PA & GMs, 11 Feb 45, subj: Establishment of Subcommittee on Pilot-less Aircraft and Guided Missiles; minutes, subcomte on P/A & GMs, 22 Jan & 5 Apr 46.

56. Ltr (lst Ind), Brig Gen A.R. Crawford, Ch, Res & Eng Div, AC/AS-4 to CG, ATSC, 25 Feb 46, subj: Bureau of Aeronautics Pilot-less Aircraft Development Program; ltrs, Col G.E. Price, Ch, Acft Projs Sect, Eng Div, AMC to Crawford, 23 Apr, 26 Apr, & 8 May 46, subj: Conflicting Guided Missile Contracts; R&R, Brig Gen W. L. Richardson, Ch, GM Div, AC/AS-3 to Res & Eng Div, AC/AS-4, 10 May 46, subj: Conflicting Guided Missile Contract; ltr, Crawford to CG, AMC, l0 May 46, subj: Conflicting Guided Missile Contracts.

57. Ltr, Brig Gen A. R. Crawford, Ch, Res & Eng Div, AC/AS-4 to CG, AMC, 21 May 46, subj: AAF Guided Missiles Development Program; rpt, Prepared Briefing for General Aurand, 12 Jul 46.

58. Minutes, Subcomte on P/A & GMs, 19 Sep & 17 Oct 45.

59. Washington Post, 9 Oct46; copy of presentation by R/Adm D.V. Gallery, Asst CNO (GMs), 7 Dec 46.

60. Presentation by Gallery, 7 Dec 46.

61. Memo for Record by Col M. C. Young, Ch, GM Br, AC/AS-4, 8 Jan 47, subj: Recent Navy Attitude; minutes, GM Subcomte, Aero Bd, 6 Mar 47; ltr, Brig Gen W. L. Richardson, Ch, GM & Air Def Div, AC/AS-3 to GG, AGF, 16 Jul 47, subj: Military Characteristics for Guided Missiles; ltr (1st Ind), Lt Col J. E. Pederson, Asst AAG to CG, AAF, 22 Jul 47, subj: Military Characteristics for Guided Missiles; R&R, Brig Gen T.S. Power, Dep AC/AS-3 to Actg DCG, 29 Jul 47, subj: Military Characteristics for Guided Missiles (with attached joint AAF-Navy ltr to Aero Bd,, 29 Jul 47, signed by Lt Gen H. S. Vandenberg and to be signed by Navy rep).

62. R&R, Brig Gen W. L. Richardson, Ch, GM & Air Def Div, AC/AS-3 to Res and Eng Div, AC IAS-4, 8 Jan 47, subj: Joint Meeting with AGF and Navy Guided Missile Personnel; R&R, Richardson, Ch, GM Gp, DCS/O to Reqs Div, Dir/T&R, 3 Dec 47, subj: Incorporation of AF Requirement for Air-to-Underwater Guided Missiles in Navy Project KINGFISHER; ltr, Adm D.C. Ramsey, Vice CNO to CG, AAF, 17Apr 47, no subj.; ltr, Gen Carl Spaatz, CG, AAF to Vice CNO, 2 May 47, no subj.

63. Ltr, Spaatz to Vice CNO, 2 May 47; ltr, Adm D.C. Ramsey, Vice CNO to CG, AAF, 19 May 47, no subj; R&R, Power to Actg DCG, AAF, 29 Jul 47.

CHAPTER III

1. Memo, Brig Gen R.G. Moses, AC/S, G-4 to CG, AAF, 9 Nov 42, subj: Controlled Missiles; extract, Bimonthly Rpt, Div 5 to NDRC, 15 Feb 43.

2. JNWE Dir 32/D, 16 Jan45, subj: Formation of a Guided Missiles Committee.

3. Ibid.; memo, Brig Gen W.A. Borden, Dir, NDD to CG, AAF, 17 Jan 45, subj: Formation of Guided Missile Committee Under the Joint Committee on New Weapons and Equipment; memo, Brig Gen P. W. Timberlake, DC/AS to Borden, 30 Jan 45, subj: Army Air Forces Membership on Guided Missiles Committee Under the Joint Committee on New Weapons and Equipment; draft staff summary sheet, Borden to C/S, 13 Feb 45; memo, Maj Gen E. M. Powers, Dep AC/AS, M&S to CG, AAF, 14 Feb 45, subj: AAF Representation on Guided Missiles Committee.

4. Memo, Brig Gen H.I. Hodes, Asst DC/S to CG, AAF, 15 Feb 45, subj: Secretariat for JNW Guided Missile committee; memo, Gen H.H. Arnold, CG, AAF to C/S, 24 Feb 45, subj: Secretariat for JNW Guided Missile Committee; memo, Brig Gen J. F. Phillips, Ch, Mat Div, AC/AS, M&S to AC/AS, M&S, 26 Feb 45, subj: Guided Missiles Committee Established as an Agency of

Joint Committee on New Weapons and Equipment; memo Lt Gen B. M. Giles, Dep Comdr, AAF to c/s, 9 Mar 45, subj: Secretariat for JNW Guided Missiles Committee; DAR, Mat Div, AC/AS, M&S, 16 Mar 45.

5. GMC 4/4, Summary Handbook of Guided Missiles, 1 Jul 45; GMC 12/1, Policy for Long Term Program, 4 Sep 45; GMC 12/9, A Proposed National Program for Development of Guided Missiles, 21 Nov 45; JCS 1620, 5 Feb 46.

6. GMC 12 /1, 4 Sep 45; GMC 12/9, 21 Nov 45.

7. JCS 1620, 5 Feb 46; JCS 1620/1, 5 Mar 46; JCS 1620/2, 14 Mar 46

8. Brief, AC/AS, Plans to CG, AAF, 21Mar 46, subj: JCS 1620; JCS 1620/3, 1 Apr 46.

9. JCS 1620/3, 1 Apr 46.

10. Memo, Bradley Dewey, Chmn, GMC to GMC Members, 13 Apr 46, subj: Allocation of Research and Development Responsibility; GMC 8/4, 14 Feb 47, Allocation of Research and Development Responsibility.

11. GMC 12/10, Report of Technical Panels, GMC, 17 Apr 46.

12. Minutes, Conference of Army Representatives to the JRDB, 27 Jan 47.

13. Ibid.; JRDB Charter, 6 Jun 46 (amended 3 Jul 46); Minutes, lst JRDB Mtg, 3 Jul 46; JRDB Dir, 15 Aug 46, Formation of a Committee on Guided Missiles; GMC 12/12, 28 Aug 46; Final Rpt of Guided Missiles Committee, JCS.

14. R&R-2, Maj Gen O.P. Weyland, AC/AS-5 to DC/AS for R&D, about 14 Aug 46, subj: Agenda of the Second Meeting of the JRDB; memo, Lt Col J.H. Smith, Exec, Policy Div, AG/AS-5 to Ch, Policy Div, 16 Oct 46, no subj; memo, Chr, Jt Mil Policy Br, Policy Div to Ch, Policy Div, AC/AS-5, 23 Oct 46, no subj.

15. GMC 8/4, 14 Feb 47; GMC 8/10, I May 47, Report by Planning Consultants.

16. GMC 8/10, 1May 47.

CHAPTER IV

1. Ltr, Maj Gen Donald Wilson, AC/AS, O, C&R to AC/AS, M, M&D, 19 Jul 44, subj: Military Characteristics for Remotely Controlled Rockets and/or Pilot-less Aircraft; ltr, Col R. C. Wilson, Ch, Dev Eng Br, Mat Div, AC/AS, M&S to CG, MC, 27 Jul 44, subj: Military Characteristics for Remotely Controllable Rockets and/or Pilot-less Aircraft, with lst Ind, Brig Gen F. O. Carroll, Ch, Eng Div, MG to CG, AAF, 22 Aug 44 and 2d Ind, Col Wilson to Dir, ATSC, 21 Sep 44; ATSC Technical Instructions (TI) 2003, 13 Nov 44; TI

2003-I, 13 Nov 44; TI 2003-2, 13 Nov 44; TI 2003-3, 13 Nov 44; TI2003-6, 4 Dec 44; TI 2003-7, 4 Dec 44.

2. Memo, Brig Gen B.E. Gates, Ch, Mgt Control to C/AS, 21 Dec 44, subj: Responsibility for Guided Missiles Program; memo, Brig Gen F.H. Smith, DC/AS to Ch, Mgt Control, 28 Dec 44, subj: Controlled Missiles; AAF HOI 2O-79, 1 Jan 45.

3. Memo, Brig Gen W-F, Mckee, Actg AC/AS, O, C&R to AC/AS, M&S, 2 Mar 45, subj: Controlled Missile Program; ltr, McKee to Pres, AAF Bd, 10 Feb 45, subj: Military Characteristics for Guided Missiles; R&R, McKee to AC/AS, M&S, 5 Apr 45, subj: Military Characteristics for Controlled Missiles; memo, Brig Gen Donald Wilson, AC/AS, O, C&R to Dr. E. L. Bowles, Special Consultant to CG, AAF, 6 Apr 45, subj: Military Characteristics for Controlled Missiles; memo, Col J. S. Mills, Dep Dir, NDD, WDSS to Col S. F. Giffin, Reqs Div, ACIAS, O, C&R, 10 Apr 45, subj: Proposed Letter to ATSC on Military Characteristics for Guided or Controlled Missiles.

4. Ltr, McKee to Pres, AAF Bd, 10 Feb 45.

5. Memo, F. R. Collbohm, Douglas Acft Co to Dr. E. L. Bowlee, Special Consultant to CG, AAF, 23 Mar 45, subj: Guided Missiles; memo, Mills to Giffin, 10 Apr 45; memo, Maj Gen Donald Wilson, AC/AS, O, C&R to Dr. Bowlee, 18 Apr 45, subj: Mr. Collbohm's Memorandum on Guided Missiles; R&R-2, Col J.G. Moore, Exec, AC/AS, M&S to AC/AS, O, C&R, 7 May 45, subj: Memorandum from Mr. Collbohm on Guided Missiles; ltr, Maj Gen E. M. Powers, AG/AS-4 to CG, ATSC, 10 Sep 45, subj: Goals for Long Term Guided Missiles Program.

6. Ltr, Powers to ATSC, 10 Sep 45.

7. Memo, Brig Gen A. R. Crawford, Ch, Prod Div, AC/AS-4 to Maj Gen E. M. Powers, AC IAS-4, 13 Sep 45, subj: AAF Long Term Guided Missiles Program; ltr, Powers to CG, ATSC, 18 Sep 45, subj: AAF Long Term Guided Missiles Program.

8. Memo, Lt Col L. T. Bradbury, Actg Ch, Eng Br to Brig Gen A. R. Crawford, Ch, Res & Eng Div, AC/AS-4, 11Oct 45, subj: Lack of High Level Participation at A. T. S. C. in Preparing the Guided Missiles Program.

9. Ltr (2d Ind), Brig Gen A.R. Crawford, Ch, Res & Eng Div, AC/AS-4 to CG, ATSC, 8 Nov 45, subj: Information for Joint Chiefs of Staffs Guided Missile Committee.

10. Memo, Lt Col L. T. Bradbury, Actg Ch, Eng Br to Brig Gen A. R. Crawford, Ch, Prod Div, AC/AS-4, 22 Sep 45, subj: Guided Missiles Investigation of A.A.F. Facilities by Secretariat, GMC, JCS; ltr, Maj Gen H. J. Knerr, CG, ATSC to CG, AAF, 26 Nov 45, subj: AAF Long Term Guided Missiles Program; ltr (3d Ind), unsigned, ATSC to CG, AAF., 28 Nov 45, subj: Information for Joint Chiefs of staffs' Guided Missile Committee.

11. Ltr, Knerr to CG, AAF, 26 Nov 45; ltr, Col G.E. Pricer C, Acft Projs Sect, Eng Div, ATSC to CG, AAF, 5 Dec 45, subj: Progress Report on Current Guided Missiles Program; ltr, Col G. F. Smith, Ch, Svc Eng Subdiv, Eng Div, ATSC to 29 acft companies, 29 Jan 46, subj: Proposal for Fighter Launched Air-to-Air Supersonic Pilot-less Aircraft Research Program.

12. Ltrs, Col G.E. Price, Ch, Acft Projs sect, Eng Div, AMC to GG, AAF, 12 Feb 46, 11 Mar 46, & 10 May 46, subj: Progress Report on Current Guided Missiles Program; ltr, Col G. F. Smith, Ch, Svc Eng Subdiv, Eng Div, AMC to CG, AAF, 29 Mar 46, subj: AMC Guided Missile Program.

13. See note above; ltr, Brig Gen A. R. Crawford, Ch, Res & Eng Div, AC/AS-4 to CG, AMC, 26 Jul 46, subj: Military Characteristics of Guided Missiles; ltr (1st Ind), Col G.E. Price, Chr Acft Projs Sect, Eng Div, AMC to CG, AAF, 20 Aug 46; Statements of Military Characteristics for 50-mile Air-to-surface Missile, 3 Sep 46, and for Air-to-Underwater Missile, 5 Sep 46.

14. See note above; interview with V. S. Roddy, Ch Engr, Dir/R&D, DCS/D, 20 Jun 58; see also Mary R. Self, The Development Of Guided Missiles, 1946-1950, fn 12, p 129.

15. Memo for Record by Col M. C. Young, Ch, GM Br, Res & Eng Div, AC/AS-4, 27 Dec 46, subj: Wright Field Recommendations for Guided Missile Projects to be Dropped; ltr, Col G. E. Price, Ch, GM Sect, Eng Div, AMC to Glenn L. Martin Co, 31 Dec 46, subj: Change in Scope of Contract; memo for record by GM Br, AC/AS-4, 1 Jan 47, no subj; msg, Price to CG, AAF, 2 Jan47, no subj; memo for record by GM Br, AC/AS-4, 7 Jan47, no subj; msg WAR-89244, CG, AAF to CG, AMC, 8 Jan 47, no subj; ltr, Lt Gen N.F. Twining, CG, AMC to CG, AAF, 25 Mar 47, subj: AAF Guided Missile R&D Program – Where We Stand.

16. R&R, Brig Gen T.S. Power, Dep AC/AS-3 to AC/AS-4, 17 Feb 47, subj: Military Characteristics for Guided Missiles and Associated Equipment.

17. Ltr, Maj Gen C.E. LeMay, DC/AS for R&D to CG, AMC, L7 Mar 47,subj: Military Characteristics for Guided Missiles and Associated Equipment.

18. Ltr, Twining to CG, AAF, 25 Mar 47; Ltr, Brig Gen B.W. Chidlaw, DCG, Eng, AMC to CG, AAF, 6 May 47, subj: AAF Guided Missiles Program.

19. R&R, Maj Gen C.E. LeMay, DC/AS for R&D to AC/AS-4 15 Jun 47, subj: Current and Revised AAF Guided Missile Program; memo, Col M. F. Cooper, AAF Member, GM Subcmte, Aero Bd to GM Subcmte, 20 Jun 47, subj: Revised AAF Guided Missile Program.

20. Memo, Brig Gen T.S. Power, Dep AC/AS-3 to CG, AAF, 15 Jun 47, subj: Operational Requirements (Priorities) for Guided Missiles, 1947 - 1957 (with Lt Gen H. S. Vandenberg, DCG, AAF initialed approval on 18 Jun 47); R&R, Maj Gen C.E. LeMay, DC/AS for R&D to AC/AS-3, 19 Jun 47, subj: Operational Requirements (Priorities) for Guided Missiles, 1947- 1957.

21. Memo, Lt Col V. A. Stace, Ch, Special Wpns Sect to Lt Col L. T. Bradbury, Actg Ch, Eng Br, Prod Div, AC/AS-4, 8 Aug 45, subj: New Explosives and Propulsion for Guided Missiles; memo, Bradbury to Stace, 10 Aug 45, subj: New Explosives and Propulsion for Guided Missiles; R&R-2, Col G.W. McGregor, Actg Ch, GM Div, AC/AS-3 to Eng Br, Mat Div, AC IAS-4, 7 Sep 45, subj: Development of Very Large Deep Penetration Controlled Missiles; ltr, Powers to CG, ATSC, 10 Sep 45.

22. Hearing on Science Legislation for Subcmte on War Mobilization, Subcmte on Military Affairs, 18 Oct 45; R&R, Col G. W.McGregor, Actg Ch, GM Div, AC/AS-3 to AC/AS-4, 19 Oct 45, subj: Military Characteristics for Air-to-Ground Guided Missiles (with attached MC's); R&R-5, Col W.P. Fisher, Asst to DC/AS for R&D to Res & Eng Div, AC/AS-4, 28 Nov 45, subj: Military Characteristics for Air-to-Ground Guided Missiles; draft ltr, AC/AS-4 to CG, ATSC, 19 Dec 45, no subj: ltr, Brig Gen A. R. Crawford, Ch, Res & Eng Div, AC/AS-4 to CG, ATSC, 9 Jar. 45, subj: Development Study for Air-to-Ground Guided Missile.

23. Ltr, Brig Gen L. C. Craigie, Ch, Eng Piv, AT$C to Maj Gen L. R. Groves, Manhattan Dist, 6 Dec 45, subj: AAF Pilot-less Aircraft Program.

24. Ltr (lst Ind), Brig Gen A. R. Crawford, Ch, Res & Eng Div, AC/AS-4 to CG, ATSC, 16 Dec 45, subj: AAF Pilot-less Aircraft Program; ltr, Crawford to CG, ATSC, 7 Dec 45, subj: Nuclear Energy Data for AAF Research and Development Purposes; ltr, Crawford to CG, ATSC, 18 Feb 46, subj: Fundamental and Applied Research and Development into Nuclear Energy by Manhattan District for the AAF; memo rpt, TSEAC 4-4485-1-6, Preliminary Design Study, Air-to-Ground Missile ATSC Design 1058, by Acft Lab, AMC, l Mar 46; ltr, CoI J.G. Moore, Dep AC/AS-4 to CG, AMC, 29 Mar 46, subj: Development of Air-to-Ground Guided Missile.

25. Ltr, Brig Gen L. C. Craigie, Ch, Eng Div, AMC to CG, AAF, 4 Apr 46, subj: Development of Air-to-Ground Guided Missiles; R&R, Brig Gen A.R. Crawford, Ch, Res & Eng Div, AC/AS-4 to DC/AS for R&D, 11 Apr 46, subj: Guided Missiles to Carry Existing Atomic Bomb; ltr, Maj Gen C.E. LeMay, DC/AS for R&D to CG, Manhattan Dist, 17 Apr 46, subj: Development of Air-to-Ground Missiles; ltr, Craigie to CG, AAF, 9 May 46, subj: Development of Air-to-Ground Missiles.

26. Ltr, Brig Gen A. R. Crawford, Ch, Res & Eng Div, AC/AS-4 to CG, AMC, 12 Jun 46, subj: Development of Air-to-Ground Missiles; ltr, Col G. E|. Price, Ch, Acft Projs Sect, Eng Div, AMC to CG, Manhattan Dist, 18 Jul 46, subj: Security Classification; memo, Crawford to DC/AS for R&D, 28 Aug 46, subj: Coordination of Information on Atomic Bomb.

27. Ltr, Brig Gen L. C. Craigie, Ch, Eng Div, AMC to CG, Manhattan Dist, 4 Sep 46, subj: Request for Information for Use of Atomic War-head in Guided Missiles (with lst Ind, Maj Gen C.E. LeMay, DC/AS for R&D to Manhattan Dist, 4 Oct 46ll'Ltr, Brig Gen A. R. Crawford, Ch, Res & Eng Div, AC /AS-4 to CG, AMC, l Nov 46, subj: Bomb Installation Drawings (with lst Ind, Brig

Gen J. S. Stowell, Ch/Admin, AMC to CG, AAF, 27 Nov 461; ltr, Col J. R. Sutherland, Eng Div Coordinating Office for the Manhattan Project, AMC to CG, Manhattan Proj, 5 Nov 46, subj: Pilot-less Aircraft Guided Missile (with Ist Ind, Col H.G. Bunker, Asst DC/AS for R&D to CG, Manhattan Dist, 22 Nov 46); ltr, Craigie to CG, AAF, 4 Dec 46, subj: Security on Manhattan Project.

28. Ltr, Maj Gen L. R. Groves, Manhattan Proj to CG, AAF, 12 Dec 46, subj: Installation Drawings and Data Relating to A-Bomb and Atomic warhead for Controlled Missiles.

29. R&R, Col J.R. Sutherland, Eng Div Coordinating Office for Manhattan Proj to Col G.E. Price, Ch, Acft Projs Sect, Eng Div, AMC, 24 Jan 47, subj: Information for Project Mastiff.

30. Ltr, Maj Gen L. C. Craigie, Ch, Eng Div, AMC to CG, AAF, 29 Jan 47, subj: Air-to-Surface Guided Missile with Atomic Warhead.

31. Draft ltr, Brig Gen A.R. Crawford, Ch, Res & Eng Div, AC/AS-4 to GG, AMC, 11 Feb 47, subj: Air-to-Surface Guided Missile with Atomic Warhead (not sent); ltr, Crawford to CG, AMC, 25 Feb 47, subj: Air-to-Surface Guided Missile with Atomic Warhead; ltr, Lt Gen L.H. Brereton, Chmn, MLC to CG, AAF, 14 Feb 47, subj: Atomic Bomb Installation Information.

32. Mil Characteristics, Air-to-Surface Guided Missile, 28 Oct 47; memo rpt, MCREXA4-4486-2-1, Design Study, Air-to-Surface Guided Missile, AMC Design 1061, by Acft Lab, AMC, 14 May 48; ltr, Lt Col J.H. Carter, Ch, GM Br, Eng Div, AMC to C/S,USAF, 13 Aug 48, subj: Design Study for "Mastiff" Type Air-to-Surface Guided Missile.

33. Memo for Record by Col M.F. Cooper, GM Br, Res & Eng Div, AC/AS-4, 26 Feb 47, no subj: R&R, Col M.C. Young, GM Br, Dir/R&D, DCS/M to GM Gp, 27 May 49, subj: MASTIFF Project MX-983.

34. Ltr, Lt Gen N.F. Twining, CG, AMC to GG, AAF, 28 Aug 47, subj: AMC Participation in the Atomic Energy Program.

35. Memo, Col M. C. Young, Ch, GM Br to Maj Gen L. C. Craigie, Ch, Res & Eng Div, AC/AS-4, 12 Sep 47, subj: Delays in Obtaining In-formation from Atomic Energy Commission.

36. R&R, Col M.F. Cooper, Ch, GM Br to Propulsion & Eqpt Br, Res & Eng Div, AC/AS-4, 24 Feb 47, subj: Air-to-Surface Missile Carrying Atomic warhead.

CHAPTER V

1. PL 253, 80th Cong, The National Security Act of 1947, 26 Jul 47.

2. Memo of Agreement, Agreement on Air and Army Positions for Separation of Air Force and Army, 25 Aug 47, by Maj Gen E. E. Partridge, AC/AS-3 and Lt Gen C. P. Hall, G-3, WDGS; Agreement, Army-Air Force Agreements as to the Initial Implementation of the National Security Act of.1947, 15 Sep 47; memo, J.V. Forrestal, SOD to Secy/Army & Secy/AF, no subj, 14 Oct 47; EO 9877, 26 Jul 47, Functions of the Armed Forces.

3. The Forrestal Diaries, ed by Walter Millis, Viking Press, NewYork, October 51

4. Ibid., 378, 389-393; EO 9950, 21 Apr 48, Functions of the Armed Forces and the Joint Chiefs of Staff; memo for record by JCS, 26 Mar 48, and approved by SOD, 1 Jul 48, see AF Bul No 3, 4 Aug 48.

5. Agreement . . . as to the Initial Implementation, 15 Sep 47.

6. Ltr, Lt Gen H.S. Aurand, Dir/S,S,&P, USA to C/S USAF, 3 Mar 48, subj: Guided Missiles Research and Development, Department of the Army; ltr (1st Ind), Lt Gen H.A. Craig, DCS/M, USAF to C/S, USA, 20 Mar 48, subj: Guided Missiles Research and Development, Department of the Army; Minutes of Meeting, Army and Air Force Guided Missile Conference Group, 26 May 48; Jt Army-Air Force Adjustment Reg 1-11-27, 22 Jun 48.

7. RDB 1/5, 18 Dec 47; Annual Rpt of Exec Secy, RDB, 17 Sep 48.

8. Statement, Dr V. Bush, Chmn, RDB to Presidential Air Policy Commission, 28 Oct, 47.

9. GMC 1/3, 23 Jan 48; Minutes of 10th GMC Mtg, 3 Feb 48.

10. GMC 50/5, 9 Jun 48.

11. Ltr, Brig Gen W.L. Richardson, AF Member, GMC to Chmn, GMC, 13 Aug 48, no subj; ltr, Brig Gen F.O. Carroll, AF Member, GMC, to Chmn, GMC, 1 Aug 48, no subj.

12. Minutes of 13th GMC Mtg, 15 Sep 48; ltr, Brig Gen W.L. Richardson, AF Member, GMC to Chmn, GMC, 18 Nov 48, subj: Comments on Report of the GMC.

13. Minutes of 14th GMC Mtg, 15 Dec 48; GMC 36/13, 15 Dec 48; RDB 188/1, 16 Dec 48; RDB 133/2, 16 Dec 48.

14. Agreement . . . as to the Initial Implementation, 15 Sep 47.

15. Compare the draft agreement of 25 Aug 47 with the final agreement of 15 Sep 47.

16. Agreement . . . as to the Initial Implementation, 15 Sep 47.

17. Air Staff Summary Sheet, Maj Gen S. E. Anderson, Dir/P&O to DCS/O, C/S, and SAF, 28 Jun 48, subj: Operational Employment of Guided Missiles; memo, Col C. B. Westover, Asst Exec, OSAF. to Maj Gen W.F. McKee, Asst DCS/O, 14 Jul 48, no subj; memo, Col M. G. Young, Ch, GM Br, Eng Div to

Maj Gen L. C. Craigie, Dir/R&D, DCS/M, 14 Jul 48, subj: Operational Employment of Guided Missiles.

18. Memo, Lt Col R. C. Richardson, JSPG, JCS to Brig Gen R. C. Lindsey, Ch, Policy Div, Dir/P&O, 11 Jun 48, subj: Guided Missile Development.

19. Memo, Col J.W. Sessums, Exec, Dir/R&D to Maj Gen L. G. Craigie, Dir, R&D, and Lt Gen H.A. Craig, DCS/M, 30 Jul 48, subj: Guided Missile Development.

20. Memo, Lt Gen H.A. Craig, DCS/M to Maj Gen S.E. Anderson, Dir/P&O, 4 Aug 48, subj: Guided Missile Development; memo, Anderson to Lt Gen Lauris Norstad, DCS/O, 6 Aug 48, subj: Guided Missile Development; memo, Brig Gen W. L. Richardson, Ch, GM Gp, DCS/O to Gen J. T. McNarney NME Mgt Cmte, 13 Aug 48, subj: Guided Missile Development; memo, McNarney to Richardson, 16 Nov 48, no subj.

21. Memo, E. F. Sweetser, Dir/Panels, GMC to Dr L. R. Hafstad, Chmn, GMC, 5 Apr 48, subj: Air Force Practices Affecting the Guided Missiles Program; ltr, K.F. Kellerman, Exec Dir, GMC to Dr W.A. McNair, TEG, GMC, 9 Apr 48, no subj; Minutes of 12th GMC Mtg, 17 Jun 48; Minutes of 13th GMC Mtg, 15 Sep 48.

22. Memo, Sweetser to Hafstad, 5 Apr 48; Minutes of 12th GMC Mtg, 17 Jun 48; Minutes of 13th GMC Mtg, 15 Sep 48; ltr, K.F. Kellerman, Exec Dir, GMC to Exec Secy, RDB, 15 Sep 48, subj: Committee on Guided Missiles Action with Regard to the National Guided Missiles Program.

23. Memo, E. F. Sweetser, Dir/Panels, GMC to F. H. Richardson, Dep Exec Secy, RDB, 30 Nov 48, subj: Weakness in the Guided Missiles Program.

24. Ibid. memo, I..H. Richardson, Dep Exec Secy, RDB to Dr K.T. Compton, Chmh, RDB, 30 Nov 48, subj: Weaknesses in the Guided Missiles Program; Memo for record by Brig Gen J. F. Phillips, AF Secy, RDB, 3 Nov 48, subj: Comments on Annual Report of Executive Secretary, RDB.

25. Minutes of 17th RDB Mtg, 16 Dec 48; memo, Dr K. T. Compton, Chmn, RDB to Chmn, GMC, 25 Jan49, subj: GM 36/13, Report of the Committee on Guided Missiles; Minutes of 15th GMC Mtg, 10 Feb 49; GMC 36/2l, 1Apr 49, Report of Special Ad Hoc Subcommittee on National Guided Missiles Program Planning.

26. GMC 32/21, 1 Apr 49; memo, Lt Col C.H. Terhune, Dep Ch, GM Br, Eng Div to Brig Gen D.L. Putt, Dir/R&D, DCS/M, 7 Mar 49, subj: Review of the National Guided Missile Program; ltr, V/Adm A.W. Radford, VCNO to C/S, USAF, 17 Jan 49,subj: Air Force Collateral Functions with Respect to the Navy"

27. Memo, Terhune to Putt, 7 Mar 49; memo, Col J.W. Sessums, Exec, Dir/R&D to Brig Gen D. L. Putt, Dir/R&D, about 8 Mar 49, no subj.

28. TEG 919, 25 Mar 49; memo, Lt Col C.H. Terhune, AF Member GMC to Chmn Special Ad Hoc Subcmte on Natl GM program planning. 25 Mar 49, no subj; memo for record by Lt Col C.H.Terhuner, Dep Ch, GM Br, Dir/R&D, 25 Mar 49, no subj; Minutes of l6th GMC Mtg, 14 Apr 49.

29. Memo, Gen J. T. McNarney & Brig Gen D.L. Putt, AF Members, RDB to Chmn RDB, 20 Apr 49, subj: Committee on Guided Missiles Recommendations Regarding FY 1950 Funds; Minutes of 21st RDB Mtg, 5 May 49; memo, Dr K. T. Compton, Chmn, RDB to Depts of Army, Navy & AF, 10 May 49, subj: Changes to be Made to Current Guided Missiles Program.

30. Presn, Guided Missiles, by a team under Brig Gen W. L. Richardson, Ch, GM Gp, DCS/O to USAF Acft & wpns Bd, 27-30 Jan 48; Minutes, USAF Acft & Wpns Bd, 27-30 Jan 48; memo, Secy, Acft & Wpns Bd to C/S, USAF, 10 Feb 48; subj: Summary Minutes of Second Meeting, USAF Aircraft and Weapons Board (with lst Ind (of approval)), Maj Gen W.F. McKee, Asst VC/S to USAF Acft & Wpns Bd, 3 Mar 48.

31. Minutes, Board of Senior Officers, 29-31 Dec 48 & 3-6 Jan 49

CHAPTER VI

1. Ltr, Lt Col F.D. Roberts, Asst AG, AFF to Dir/Log, USA, 19 Feb 49, subj: Military Characteristics for Surface-to-Air (Long-Range) Guided Missiles; R&R, Col G.F. McGuire, Asst Ch, Ops Div, Dir/P&O to GM Div, GM Gp, DCS/O, 3 Mar 49, subj: Army Field Forces Military Characteristics for SAM; R&R, McGuire to GM Div, 16 Mar 49, subj: AFF Military Characteristics for SAM (Long-Range) memo, Gordon Gray, Actg Secy/Army to SOD, 16 May 49, subj: Assignment of Responsibility for Guided Missiles operations and Development.

2. Memo, Gray to SOD , 16 May 49.

3. Memo, Louis Johnson, SOD to JCS, 25 May 49, subj: Assignment of Responsibility for Guided Missile Operations; memo, Johnson to RDB 25 May 49, subj: Assignment of Responsibility for Research and Development in the Field of Guided Missiles; SN to JSPC, 27 May 49, subj: Assignment of Responsibility for Guided Missile Operations; SN to JSPG, 30 May 49, subj: Assignment of Responsibility for Guided Missile Operations.

4. JSPC 902/4/D.

5. JSPG Rpt 902/18, 8 Aug 49.

6. Ibid. ; ASSS, Maj Gen S. E. Anderson, Dir/P&O to DCSrs, C/S, & SAF, 22 Jul 49, subj: Policy Statement on Service Responsibilities for New Weapons.

7. Memo, Brig Gen P. M. Hamilton, AF Member, JSPG to Brig Gen Joseph Smith, AF Member, JSPC, 11 Aug 49, subj: Assignment of Responsibility for

Guided Missile Operations (JSPC 902/18) memo, Smith to JSPC, about 11 Aug 49, subj: Assignment of Responsibility for Guided Missile Operations (JSPC 902/19); JSPC 902/4/D.

8. Memo, R/Adm C.D. Glover, USN Member, JSPG to JSPG, 19 Aug 49, no subj; memo, Brig Gen P. M. Hamilton, AF Member, JSPG to Brig Gen J. Smith, AF Member, JSPC, about 23 Aug 49, subj: Assignment of Responsibility for Guided Missile Operations; memo, R/Adm W.F. Boone, USN Member, to JSPC, ?4 Aug4l, subj: Assignment of Responsibility for Guided Missile Operations; memo, Col C. G. Goodrich, Ch, Domestic Br, Plans Dir to Maj Gen S. E. Anderson, Dir/P&O, I Sep 49, subj: Definition of the term "Operational Responsibility" in Connection with JSPC 902/18.

9. Memo, W.S. Symington, SAF to L. Johnson, SOD, 19 Aug 49, subj: Assignment of Responsibility for Guided Missile Operations.

10. Ibid.

11. Memo, Maj Gen S. E. Anderson, Dir/P&O to W. S. Symington, SAF 6 Sep 49, subj: DOD Policy Governing Assignment of Operational and Developmental Responsibilities for New Weapons; extract from memo by Dir/P&O, 23 Sep 49, subj: Matters of Interest to the AF Discussed at the AFPC Meeting of September 20, 1949; memo, Capt W.G. Lalor, Secy/JCS to JSPC, 23 Sep 49, subj: Operational Control of Guided Missiles; JSPC 902/4 /D.

12. Memo, Anderson to Symington, 6 Sep 49; memo, Maj Gen J. Smith, Dep Dir/P&O to DCS/O, 23 Sep 49, subj: Assignment of Responsibility for Guided Missile Operations; memo, Smith to JSPC, 26 Sep 49, subj: Assignment of Responsibility for Guided Missile Operations (JSPC 902/18).

13. Memo, Smith to JSPC, 26 Sep 49.

14. Memo, Brig Gen C. J. R. Schuyler, Army Member, JSPC to JSPC, 26 Sep 49, subj: Assignment of Responsibility for Guided Missile Operations (JSPC 902/18). Maj Gen S. E. Anderson, Dir/P&0 to C/S 29 Sep 49, subj: Assignment of Responsibility for Guided Missile Operations.

15. Memo, JSPC to JCS, 28 Sep 49, subj: Assignment of Responsibility for Guided Missile Operations; JCS 1620/8; note by Secy/JGS, 30 Sep 49; memo, Col G.W. Martin, OSAF to W.S. Symington, SAF., 30 Sep 49, no subj; memo, Maj Gen S.E. Anderson, Dir/P&O to Lt Gen Laurie Norstad, AF Ops Dep, JCS, about j Oct 49, subj: Assignment of Operational Control of Guided Missiles (SM-1981-49).

16. Directive, JSPC to JSPG, 3 Oct 49, subj: Assignment of Operational Control of Guided Missiles; memo, Capt W.G. Lalor, Secy/JCS to Ops Dept, JCS, 31 Oct 49, subj: Operational Control of Guided Missiles.

17. Extract of memo by Dir/P&O, 7 Nov 49, subj: Results of the Meeting of the Operations Deputies; 1620/12.

18. 1620/12 memo, Maj Gen S.E. Anderson, Dir/P&O to W.S. Symington, SAF, 6 Dec 49, subj: DoD Policy Governing Assignment of Operational and Developmental Responsibilities for New Weapons; extract of memo by Dir/P&O, subj: Significant Activities of the AFPC at its Meeting of 6 December 1949.

19. Memo, Anderson to Symington, 6 Sep 49.

20. Memo, Gray to SOD, 16 May 49; memo, Johnson to RDB, 25 May 49; memo, F.H. Richardson, Dep Exec Secy, RDB to GMC, 31May 49, subj: Assignment of Responsibility for Research and Development in Field of Guided Missiles; draft memo, GMC to RDB, 31 May49, subj: Assignment of Responsibility for Research and Development in Field of Guided Missiles; memo, R. F. Rinehart, Exec Secy, RDB to SOD, 2 Jun 49, subj: Assignment of Responsibilities for Research and Development in the Field of Guided Missiles; memo, Rinehart to JCS, 13 Jun 49, subj: Assignment of Responsibilities for Research and Development in the Field of Guided Missiles; Minutes of 17th GMC Mtg, 16 Jun 49.

21. Memo, F.A. Darwin, Exec Dir, GMC to RDB, 5 Dec 49, subj: Assignment of Responsibilities for Research and Development in the Field of Guided Missiles.

22. Minutes of 22nd GMC Mtg, 16 Dec 49; memo, F.H. Richardson, Dep Exec secy, RDB to GMC, 13 Dec 49, subj: Assignment of Primary Responsibility for Research and Development in Field of Guided Missiles; memo, F.A. Darwin, Exec Dir, GMC to RDB, 3 Jan 50, subj: Appointment of Ad Hoc Subcommittee on Assignment of Guided Missiles Research and Development Responsibility; memo, Richardson to RDB, 13 Jan 50, subj: Assignment of Responsibilities for Research and Development in the Field of Guided Missiles; memo, Darwin to RDB, 6 Feb 50, subj: Assignment of Responsibilities for Research and Development in the Field of Guided Missiles.

23. Rpt of the Ad Hoc Subcommittee on Assignment of Responsibility for Research and Development in the Field of Guided Missiles, 31 Mar 50.

24. Staff Study, Assignment of Responsibility for Research and Development in the Field of Guided Missiles, by GMC Sec't, 17 Apr 50.

25. Minutes of 3d GMC Exec Subcmte Mtg, 24 Apr 50; memo F.A. Darwin, Exec Dir, GMC to RDB, 28 Apr 50, subj: Assignment of Responsibility for Research and Development in the Field of Guided Missiles; Minutes of 31st RDB Mtg, 17 May 50; memo, William 'Webster, Chmn, RDB to SOD, 9 Jun 50, subj: Allocation of Responsibility for Research and Development in the Field of Guided Missiles.

26. Memo, L. Johnson, SOD to Chms, RDB, 27 Jul 50, subj: Assignment of Responsibility for Research and Development in the Field of Guided Missiles.

27. Memo, W. Webster, Chmn, RDB to SOD, 9 Aug 50, subj: Assignment of Responsibility for Research and Development in the Field of Guided Missiles.

28. PL 60, 81st Cong, 11 May 49; memo, Louis Johnson, SOD to RDB, 15 Jul 49, no subj.

29. Memo, C.B. Millikan, Chmn, GMC to Chmn, RDB, 26 Aug 49, subj: Guided Missile Program.

30. Memo, K. T. Compton, Chmn, RDB to GMC, 26 Sep 49, subj: R&D Areas Where Economies Might Be Effected; memo, C. B. Millikan, Chmn, GMC to RDB, 14 Oct 49, subj: R&D Areas Where Economies Might Be Effected.

31. Memo, R. F. Rinehart, Exec Secy, RDB to Exec Dir, GMC, 28 Sep 49, subj: R&D Areas Where Economies Might Be Effected; memo, Millikan to RDB, 14 Oct 49; memo, F.H. Darwin, Exec Dir, GMC to Exec Secy, RDB, 14 Oct 49, subj: Economies Possible in the Guided Missile Program (with attached staff study, "Staff Analysis of Controversial Guided Missile Items").

32. Minutes of 26th RDB Mtg, 26 Oct 49; Minutes of 2lst GMC Mtg, 18 Nov 49; memo, R. F. Rinehart, Exec Secy, RDB to Chmn, GMC, 16 Dec 49, subj: Recommended Withdrawal of PL 24/1.

33. Memo, K.T. Compton, Chmn, RDB to SOD, 31 Oct 49, subj: Progress Report on Study of Guided Missiles program.

34 PL 24/1, Staff Study on the Guided Missile program, 25 Oct 49, by Planning Div, RDB; Minutes of 2lst GMC Mtg, 18 Nov 49; memo, C.B. Millikan, Chmn, GMC to RDB, I Dec 49, subj: Recommended Withdrawal of PL 24/1; memo, F,H. Darwin, Exec Dir, GMC to RDB, 10 Dec 49, subj: Recommended Withdrawal of PL 24/1; memo, Rinehart to Chmn, RDB, 16 Dec 49.

35. Memo, GM Br, Dir/R&D to W.S. Symington, SAF, about 20 Dec 49, no subj; memo, Lt Col W. C. Addeman, Asst Exec, Dir/P&O to DCS/M, about 28 Dec 49, subj; Significant Actions of the AFPC at its Meeting of 20 December; memo, Brig Gen D. T. Spivey, Ch, War Plans Div to Maj Gen S.E. Anderson, Dir/P&O, 9 Jan 50, no subj; Report of the Special Interdepartmental Guided Missiles Board (hereinafter cited as Stuart Rpt), Feb 50.

36. Minutes of SIGMB, 21Dec 49 & 18 Jan 50; Stuart Rpt, Feb 50.

37. Memo, Spivey to Anderson, 9 Jan 50; memo, H. C. Stuart, Asst SAF to SAF, 24 Jan 50, subj: Comments on Study of National Guided Missile Program; memo, R/Adm G.B.H. Hall, Navy Wkg Member, SIGMB to U/Secy/Navy, 27 Jan 50, subj: Evaluation of the Situation as Regards the Stuart Committee; memo, Col M. C. Young, SIGMB Recorder to H. C. Stuart, Chmn, SIGMB, 30 Jan 50, subj: Navy Remarks at Eighth Meeting of SIB and Comments Thereon; Stuart Rpt, Feb 50.

38. Memo, Spivey to Anderson, 9 Jan 50; draft memo, Maj Gen F.F. Everest, DCS/O to SAF, 10 Jan 50, subj: Assignment of Long-Range SSM Mission.

39. Stuart Rpt, Feb 50.

40 Ibid., Atch A.

41. Ibid., Atch B.

42. Ibid., Atch C.

43 Ibid., Atch D.

44. Stuart Rpt, Feb 50.

45. Ibid.; memo for record by Maj J.R. Dempsey, GM Br, Dir/R&D, 20 Feb 50, subj: Sequence of Events Concerning SIB.

46. Extract by Dir/P&O, 16 Feb 50, subj: Significant Actions of AFPC at its Meeting of 16 February 1950; memo for record by Dempsey, 20 Feb 50; Presn on Guided Missile Program by R.F. Rinehart, Exec Secy, RDB to JCS, 24 Feb 50; memo, Rinehart to Chmn, RDB, 28 Feb 50, subj: Guided Missiles Inquisition.

47. JSPC 902/47, 20 Feb 50, subj: Guided Missiles Program; Presn, Guided Missiles, Program, by S.D. Comell, Planning Div, RDB to JCS, 23 Feb 50; draft memo, JCS to SOD, 24 Feb 50, subj: Department of Defense Guided Missiles Program.

48. Draft memo, JCS to SOD, 24 Feb 50; memo, Col L. H. Dalton, Ch, Special Wpns Team, WPD to Ch, WPD, Dir/P&O, 24 Feb 50, subj: Guided Missile Program; draft memo, Maj Gen S. E. Anderson, Dir/P&O to C/S, USAF, 25 Feb 50, subj: Guided Missiles Program; memo, Dalton to Ch, WPD, 3 Mar 50, subj: JCS Action on the Guided Missile Program.

49. Memo, Secy, JS to JCS, I Mar 50, subj: Status of Agreements Reached on the Guided Missiles Program; memo, Secy, JS to Ops Deps, 10 Mar 50, subj: Guided Missiles Program; memo, Adm F. P. Sherman, CNO to JCS, 13 Mar 50, subj: Guided Missiles Program; memo, Col E. A. Romig, Special Wpns Team, WPD to Maj Gen I. H. Edwards, AF Ops Dep, 13 Mar 50, subj: Guided Missiles Program.

50. Memo, Secy, JS to JCS, 13 Mar 50, subj: Guided Missiles Program; memo, Secy, JS to JCS, 14 Mar 50, subj: Department of Defense Guided Missiles Program; memo, JCS to SOD, 15 Mar 50, subj: Department of Defense Guided Missiles Program /JCS 1620/17.

51. Stuart Rpt, Feb 50; memo, Secy, JS to JCS, 3 Mar 50; memo, Gen H.S. Vandenberg, C/S, USAF to JCS, 6 Mar 50, subj: Guided Missiles Program; memo, Secy, JS to JCS, 1 Mar 50; memo, Maj Gen S. E. Anderson, Dir/P&O to C/S, USAF, 9 Mar 50, subj: Guided Missiles Program; memo, Secy, JS to Ops Deps, 10 Mar 50; memo, Secy, JS to JCS, 14 Mar 50; memo, JCS to SOD, 15 Mar 50.

52. Memo, Anderson to C/S, USAF, 2 Mar 50.

53. Draft memo, Secy, JS to JCS, 24 Feb 50; memo, Adm F. P. Sherman, CNO to JCS, 1 Mar 50, subj: Guided Missiles Program; memo, Vandenberg to JCS, 6 Mar 50; memo, Secy, JS to JCS, 14 Mar 50; memo, JCS to SOD, 15 Mar 50.

54. Memo, JCS to SOD, 15 Mar 50,

55. Presn, US Guided Missile Program, by S.D. Cornell, Planning Div, RDB to SOD, 20 Mar 50; memo, Brig Gen D. T. Spivey, Ch, WPD to Dir/P&O, 21 Mar 50, subj: Guided Missile Program; memo, L. Johnson, SOD, to JCS, 21 Mar 50, subj: Department of Defense Guided Missiles Program.

56. Memo, T. G. Lanphier, Special Consultant to SAF to SAF, 22 Mar 50, subj: Analysis of JCS 1620/17 on Guided Missiles; rpt, Review of Guided Missiles Program, by Special Wpns Team, WPD, about 5 May 50.

57 Rpt of Technical Evaluation Group, Committee on Guided Missiles, RDB, 20 May 49; ltr, W. Webster, Chmn, RDB to Secy, JS, 21 Jul 49, subj: Establishment of a Military Basis for Guided Missile Program Planning.

58. JCS 1630/10, 5 May 48; JCS 1862/1; JCS 1862/6.

59. Ltr, Webster to Secy, JS, 21 Jul 49,

60. SN to JSPC, 29 Jul 49, subj: Establishment of a Military Basis for Guided Missile Program Planning; SN to JSPG, 3 Aug 49, subj: Establishment of a Military Basis for Guided Missile Program Planning; JSPC 902/23, 22 Aug 49; memo, Brig Gen P.M. Hamilton, AF Member, JSPG to Brig Gen J. Smith, AF Member, JSPC, I Sep 49, subj: Establishment of the Military Basis for Guided Missile Program Planning.

61. Memo, Brig Gen J. Smith, AF Member, JSPC to JSPG, about 1 Sep 49, subj: Establishment of the Military Basis for Guided Missile Program Planning; memo, R/Adm W.F. Boone, Navy Member, JSPC to JSPC, 1 Sep 49, subj: Establishment of the Military Basis for Guided Missile Program Planning; memo, Col H. Moore, AF Member, JSPG to Smith, 22 Sep 49, subj: Establishment of the Military Basis for Guided Missile Program Planning.

62. JSPC 902/25, 13 Sep 49, subj: Establishment of a Military Basis for Guided Missile Program Planning, memo, Moore to Smith, 22 Sep 49.

63. Memo, Maj Gen J" Smith, Dep Dir/P&O to C/S, USAF 23 Oct 49, subj: Establishment of a Military Basis for Guided Missile Program Planning; memo, Gen H.S. Vandenberg, C/S, USAF to JCS, 24 Oct 49, subj: Establishment of a Military Basis for Guided Missile Program Planning; JCS Decision on 1620/9, 25 Oct 49; memo, Sec, JS to RDB, 26 Oct 49, subj: Establishment of a Military Basis for Guided Missile Program Planning.

64. Memo, Maj Gen S.E. Anderson, Dir/P&O to DCS/O, 30 Oct 49, subj: Establishment of a Military Basis for Guided Missiles Program Planning (1620/9); R&R, Anderson to Asst for AE, Asst for GM & Dir/R&D, 4 Nov 49, subj: Priority of Guided Missiles; R&R-2, Asst for AE, DCS/O to Dir/P&O,

14 Nov 49, subj: Priority of Guided Missiles; R&R-2, Maj Gen D. L. Putt, Dir/R&D to Dir/P&O, 6 Dec 49, subj: Priority for Guided Missiles; memo, JCS to SOD, 30 Dec 49, subj: Guided Missiles with Atomic Warheads.

65. Presn, US Guided Missile Program, 20 Mar 50.

66. Memo for Record by V.S. Roddy, GM Br, Dir/R&D, 26 Jan 49, subj: Atomic Warheads for Guided Missiles; memo Roddy to Lt Col C. H. Terhune, Ch, GM Br, Dir/R&D, 4 Mar 49, subj: Atomic Warheads for Guided Missiles.

67. Memo, Gen O.N. Bradley, C/S, USA to JCS, 24 May 4), subj: Research and Development for Weapons for Support of Land Operations.

68. Memo, CNO, USN to JCS, 28 Jun 49, subj: Research and Development for Weapons for Support of Land Operations.

69. Memo, WPD, Dir/P&O to DCS/O, I Jun 49, subj: Research and Development for Weapons for Support of Land Operations; memo, Maj Gen S.E. Anderson, Dir/P&O to C/S, about 7 Jul 49, subj: Research and Development for Weapons for Support of Land Operations; memo, C/S, USAF to JCS, LZ Jul 49, subj: Research and Development for Weapons for Support of Land Operations.

70. Memo, C/S, USAF to JCS, 12 Jul 49; memo, JCS to RDB, 14 Jul 49, subj: Research and Development for Weapons for Support of Land Operations.

71. Memo, L. Johnson, SOD to Lt Gen J.E. Hull, Dir/WSEG, 21 Jun 49, subj: Development of Guided Missiles with Atomic Warheads; memo, Hull to C/S, USA & USAF & CNO, USN, 24 Jun 49, subj: Development of Guided Missiles with Atomic Warheads.

72. Memo, Exec Secy, RDB to JGS, 20 Jul 49, subj: Present Considerations with Regard to Guided Missiles Carrying Atomic Warheads; extract by Dir/P&O, Results of the Meeting of the Operations Deputies, 10 Nov 49.

73. Memo, Lt Gen J.E. Hull, Dir/WSEG to W. Webster, Dep to SOD for Atomic Energy Matters, 14 Sep 49, subj: Guided Missiles with Atomic Warheads (hereinafter cited as Hull Rpt).

74. Memo, L. Johnson, SOD to JGS, 29 Sep 49, subj: Guided Missiles with Atomic Warheads.

75. Memo, K. T. Compton, Chmn, RDB to JCS, 26 Oct 49, subj: Guided Missiles with Atomic Warheads; memo, Compton to SOD, 27 Oct 49, subj: Guided Missiles with Atomic Warheads; memo, R.F. Rinehart, Actg Chmn, RDB to SOD, 8 Dec 49, subj: Guided Missiles with Atomic Warheads; extract by Dir/P&O, l0 Nov 49.

76. Memo, C/S, USAF to JGS, 22Nov 49, subj: Atomic Warheads for Guided Missiles.

77. Memo, C/S, USA to JCS, 8 Dec 49, subj: Guided Missiles with Atomic Warheads.

78; Memo, Maj Gen J. Smith, AF Member, JSPC to C/S, USAF, 27 Dec 49, subj: Atomic Warheads for Guided Missiles.

79. JCS 2012/5, 28 Oct 49; memo, JCS to SOD, 30 Dec 49, subj: Guided Missiles with Atomic warheads; memo, L. Johnson, SOD to RDB, 16 Jan 50, subj: Guided Missiles with Atomic Warheads; SN to JGS, 20 Jan 50, subj: Guided Missiles with Atomic Warheads.

80. Memo, Exec Secy, RDB to GMC & CAE, 20 Dec 49, no subj; memo, Exec Secy, CAE & Exec Dir, GMC to Exec Secy, RDB, 6 Jan 50, subj: Guided Missiles with Atomic Warheads; Minutes of 23d GMC Mtg, 3 Feb 50; Minutes of.2d, RDB Ad Hoc Working Group on Guided Missiles with Atomic Warheads Mtg, 20 Feb 50; Minutes of 24th GMC Mtg, 31 Mar 50; memo, Lt Col C. H. Terhune, Chm, GM Br to Dir/R&D, 4 Apr 50, Subj: Item 3, CGM, 24 Mtg

81. Memo, C/S, USA to JCS, 22 Mar 50, subj: Artillery Delivered Atomic Weapons; memo, CNO, USN to JCS, 5 Apr 50, subj: Artillery Delivered Atomic Weapons; memo, C/S, USAF to JCS' 13 Apr 50, subj: Artillery Delivered Atomic Weapons.

82. Memo, Lt Gen LeRoy Lutes, Staff Dir, MB to JCS, 9 Sep 49, subj: Mobilization Planning for Production of Guided Missiles.

83. JSPC 902/26D, 14 Sep 49; JSPC 902/28, 27 Sep 49.

84. Memo, Brig Gen C. V. R. Schuyler, Army Member, JSPC to JSPC, 4 Oct 49, subj: Mobilization Planning for Production of Guided Missiles; memo, Col M.W. Brewster, Ch, Resources Div, Dir/P&O to AF Member, JSPC, 6 Oct 49, subj: Mobilization Planning for Production of Guided Missiles; JCS 1620/10, 21 Oct 49.

85. JCS 1620/10, 21 Oct 49; memo, JCS to MB, 2 Nov 49, subj: Mobilization Planning for Production of Guided Missiles.

86. Memo, H.E. Howard, Chmn, MB to SOD, 15 Oct 50, subj: Guided Missiles Production Planning; SM 372-50, subj: Guided Missiles Production Planning.

87. Memo, Maj Gen P. W. Timberlake, Staff Dir, MB to JCS, Secy/Army, Secy/Navy, & SAF, 24 Feb 50, subj: Guided Missiles Production Planning.

88. SN to JSPC, 1 Mar 50, subj: Guided Missiles Production Planning; JSPC 902/48D, 2 Mar 50; JSPC 902/4, 31 Mar 50; JCS 1620/19; memo, JCS to MB, RDB, & Dep Secys, 26 Apr 50, subj: Guided Missiles Production Planning.

89. Memo, Brig Gen E. C. Langmead, Dir/Mil Progs, MB to JCS & Dep Secys, 19 Apr 50, subj: Guided Missiles Production Planning; memo, Langmead to JCS et al, 1 May 50, subj: Guided Missiles Production Planning; memo, Col H.F. Skies, Office of Prod Planning MB to JCS et al, 24 May 50, subj: Guided Missiles Production Planning; memo, H.C. Stuart, Asst SAF to MB, 8 Jul 50, subj: Guided Missiles Production Planning.

90. Memo, Roscoe Seybold, Actg Chmn, MB to JCS, 30 Oct 50, subj: Adequacy of Mobilization Requirements for Guided Missiles; memo, GMIORG to JCS, 9 Nov 50, subj: Requirements Program for Guided Missiles; JCS 162O/33, 3 Jan 51.

GLOSSARY

AAFPGC	Army Air Forces Proving Ground Command
AAFTC	Army Air Forces Technical Committee
AAG	Air Adjutant General
AAM	Air-to-Air Missile
AC/AS	Assistant Chief of Air Staff
Acft	Aircraft
Admin	Administration
AEC	Atomic Energy Commission
Aero	Aeronautic & Aeronautical
AF.	Air Force
AFF	Army Field Forces
AT'PC	Armed Forces Policy Council
AG	Adjutant General
AGF	Army Ground Forces
AMC	Air Materiel Command
ASF	Army Service Forces
ASM	Air-to-Surface Missile
ASSS	Air Staff Summary Sheet
ATSC	Air Technical Service Command
BuAer	Bureau of Aeronautics
BuOrd	Bureau of Ordnance
CAE	Committee on Atomic Energy
c/As	Chief of Air Staff
CNO	Chief of Naval Operations
c/s	Chief of Staff
DAR	Daily Activity Report
DCG	Deputy Commanding General
DCS/M	Deputy Chief of Staff for Materiel
DCS/O	Deputy Chief of Staff for Operations

DF	Disposition Form
DMA	Division of Military Applications
DOD	Department of Defense
Eng	Engineering
EO	Executive Order
Eqpt	Equipment
GM	Guided Missile(s)
GMC	Guided Missiles Committee, Committee on
GMIORG	Guided Missiles Interdepartmental Operational Requirements Group
JCS	Joint Chiefs of Staff
JNWE	Joint Committee on New Weapons and Equipment
JRDB	Joint Research and Development Board
JS	Joint Staff
JSPC	Joint Strategic Plans Committee
JSPG	Joint Strategic Plans Group
Mat	Materiel
MB	Munitions Board
MC	Materiel Command
Mgt	Management
MLC	Military Liaison Committee
M, M&D	Materiel, Maintenance and Distribution
M&S	Materiel and Services
NACA	National Advisory Committee for Aeronautics
Natl	National
NDD	New Developments Division
NDRC	National Defense Research Council
NME	National Military Establishment
O, C&R	Operations, Commitments, and Requirements
OPD	Operations Division

Ord	Ordnance
OSAF	Office of the Secretary of the Air Force
OSD	Office of the Secretary of Defense
OSRD	Office of Scientific Research and Development
O&T	Operations and Training
PA	Pilot-less Aircraft
PL	Public Law
P&O	Plans and Operations
Presn	Presentation
Prog	Program
Proj	Project
RDB	Research and Development Board
Reqs	Requirements
Res	Research
R&R	Routing and Record Sheet
SAF	Secretary of the Air Force
SAM	Surface-to-Air Missile
Sect	Section
Secrt	Secretariat
Secy	Secretary
Sig	Signal
SIGMB	Special Interdepartmental Guided Missiles Board
SN	Secretary's Note
SOD	Secretary of Defense
SSM	Surface-to-Surface Missile
S, S&P	Service, Supply and Procurement
SUM	Surface-to-Underwater Missile
Svcs	Services
TEG	Technical Evaluation Group
TI	Technical Instruction
T&R	Training and Requirements

U/	Under
USA	United States Army
USAF	United States Air Force
USN	United States Navy
VC/S	Vice Chief of Staff
WD	War Department
WDGS	War Department General Staff
WDSS	War Department Special Staff
Wkg	Working
WPD	War Plans Division
Wpns	Weapons
WSEG	Weapons Systems Evaluation Group

www.ingramcontent.com/pod-product-compliance
Lightning Source LLC
Chambersburg PA
CBHW030018290326

41934CB00005B/394